LIPCHITZ
A Cubist Sculptor

Edited by Judit Geskó and Anett Somodi

LIPCHITZ
A CUBIST SCULPTOR

With contributions by Kata Bodor, Adina Kamien,
Márton Orosz and Dominika Sodics

Museum of Fine Arts, Budapest
2024

LIPCHITZ
A CUBIST SCULPTOR

Museum of Fine Arts, Budapest
21 June – 1 September 2024

CONTENTS

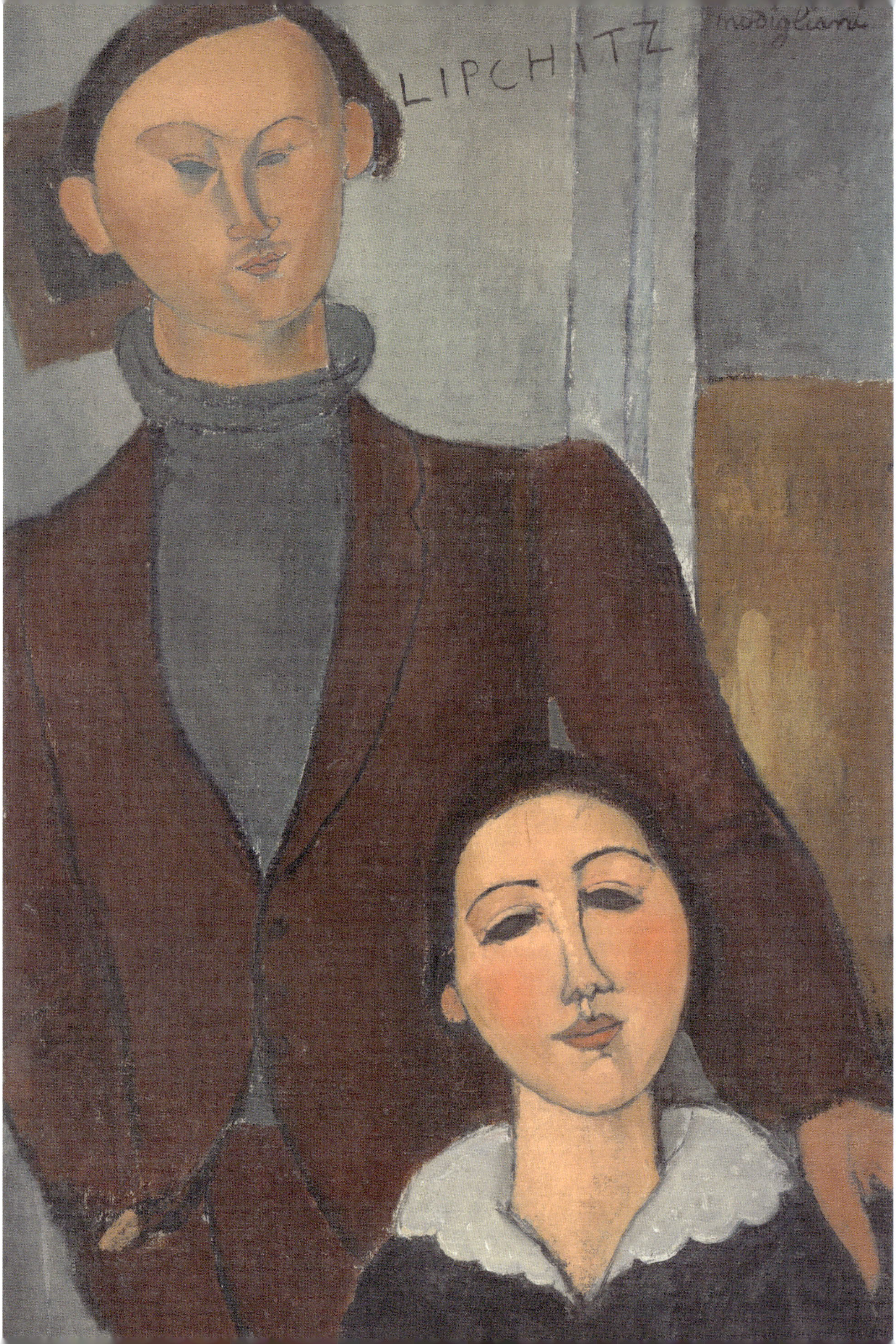
LIPCHITZ
modigliani

Judit Geskó

JACQUES LIPCHITZ, RUBIN LIPCHITZ: A MESSAGE TO BUDAPEST

Amedeo Modigliani
Jacques and Berthe Lipchitz, 1916
The Art Institute of Chicago, Chicago, Helen Birch Bartlett Memorial Collection
‹

Jacques and Rubin Lipchitz with company in front of the Chapel of the Rosary in Vence, ca. 1968
Private collection
»

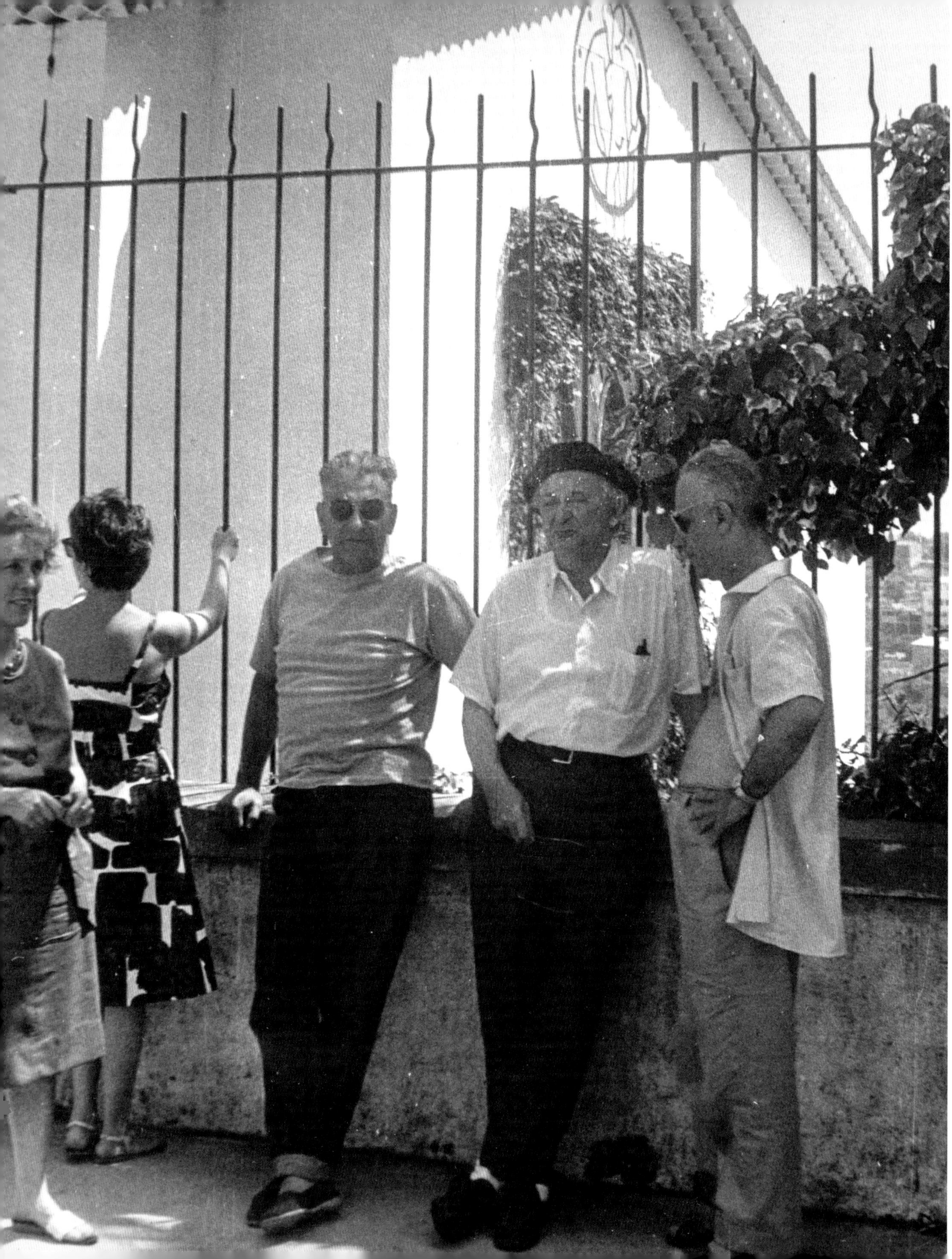

"An old photograph without a frame"
(Pierre Reverdy, *Motionless Reality*)[1]

A YOUNG CUBIST SCULPTOR

I first met Rubin Lipchitz (1906–1993) in Paris in spring 1984. Rubin's elder brother, fifteen years his senior, was the world-famous, Lithuanian-Jewish-born sculptor Jacques Lipchitz (1891–1973) (figs. 1–2), who lived and worked in France, the USA, and Italy. I became acquainted with Rubin through his contacts in Budapest. The elderly gentleman was blessed with extreme warmth towards people and the matters of the world, and since his brother's passing in 1973, he had passionately watched over the artist's legacy in sculpture, printmaking, and drawing, as well as his library.[2]

1 Druskieniki,
early 20th century
Archive postcard

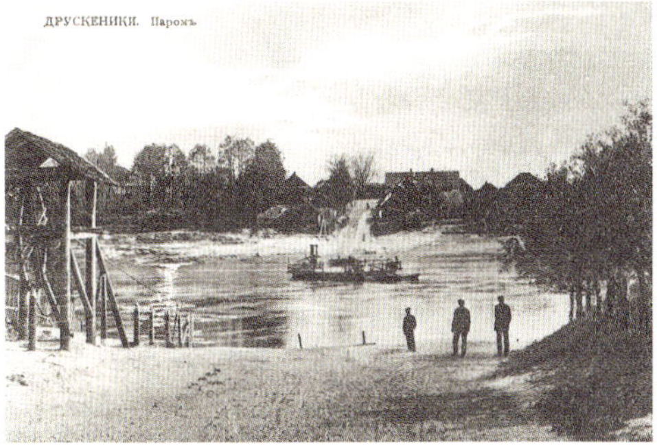

The sculptor Jacques Lipchitz is not so well-known in Hungary, which is why this exhibition of his work, in the Michelangelo Hall on the ground floor of the historically styled building of the Museum of Fine Arts, Budapest, is of such great significance.

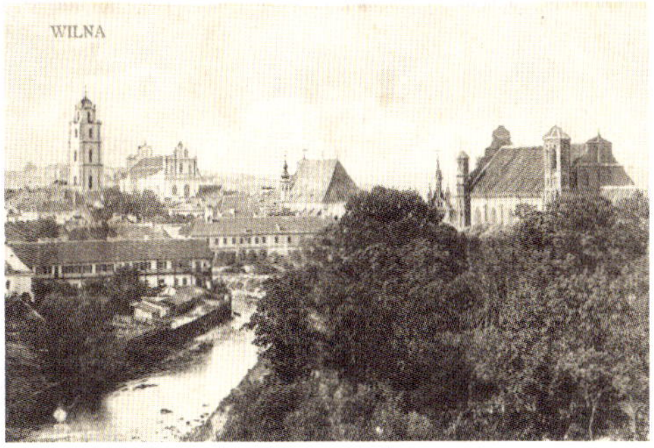

2 Panorama of Vilna (Vilnius),
ca. 1910
Archive postcard

In 1909 Lipchitz left Lithuania for Paris (fig. 3), arriving there just as exponents of analytical cubism were starting to produce paintings, collages and sculptures in the exciting new style, with figures and objects depicted broken down into pieces (1910–1912). The details were then rearranged together in the plane. In subsequent years, from 1913 onwards, they abandoned the simultaneous presentation of different perspectives and stripped the individual elements of their original meaning. The constituent parts were accorded equal value. What remained important was the composition, the intent to construct image and form. Showing things from a single viewpoint came to an end. The masters of modernism, the cubists among them, followed the twentieth-century approach to science and philosophy and thought in terms of four-dimensional spacetime. The sculptures Jacques Lipchitz made in the 1910s and 1920s (cats. 1–2) were fused with hope for a new society, but later, beginning in the 1930s, his work became filled with ominous forebodings about the changes taking place in politics and in European societies, changes that are also reflected in his later works. Exponents of expressionism, surrealism, and other movements born around the same time, searching for ways of expressing their longing for freedom, also studied the dramatic works of nineteenth-century French romantics, notably Eugène Delacroix (1798–1863) and Théodore Géricault (1791–1824). Vision and imagination were often intertwined with historical, mythological, and dreamlike events. Lipchitz's style also underwent a change when he was around forty years old. Due to the political threats that posed a terrible danger to avantgarde art, and following the invasion of German troops, he fled initially to the South of France, before resettling on the other side of the Atlantic in summer 1941. In his first year in New York, he found a gallery and a foundry, and he began to work once more. In 1946, on his first post-war visit to Paris, the French president awarded him the Légion d'Honneur for his decades-long contribution to art.

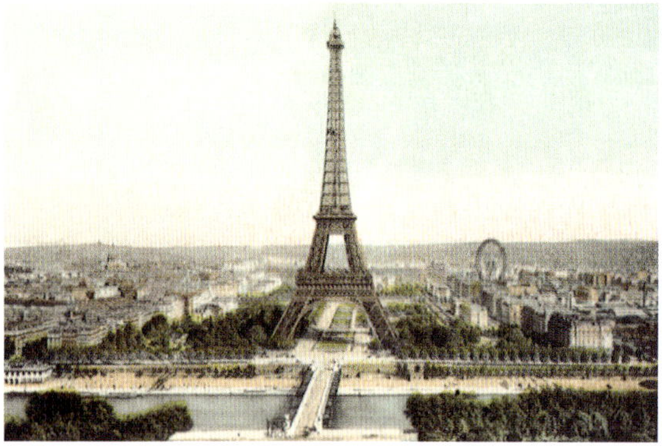

3 View of the Eiffel Tower, Paris, 1910

The master's art collection was unfortunately destroyed in a fire at his New York atelier. Many of his books too fell victim to the flames, but the volumes he kept in his studio in Hastings-on-Hudson, an hour's train ride from New York City (fig. 4) — monographs and catalogues on Théodore Géricault —, have for some time now been awaiting rediscovery in Budapest, in the Collection of International Art after 1800 at the Museum of Fine Arts. Certain answers are also awaited: Why did Jacques Lipchitz find it so important to deal with Géricault, the great French romantic painter? What could these books, with their drawings and illustrations, reveal about the secret creative thoughts and ideas that occurred to this sculptor of Eastern European origin as he studied the drama-filled œuvre of this French painter, active a century before him? What could he have talked about to his friend, the painter Boris Taslitzky (1911–2005), born in Paris to Russian émigré parents, who painted Jacques Lipchitz's magnificent bust of Géricault (figs. 5a and 5b) in emulation of the type of picture first popularised in 1642 by the baroque artist Philippe de Champaigne (1602–1674). The latter's famous triple bust of Cardinal de Richelieu (1585–1642), showing the prelate and statesman from three different angles (National Gallery, London), has for centuries exemplified how to examine the complex character of the sitter (fig. 6).

In 1977, four years after the death of Jacques Lipchitz, an anthology of key documents from the cubist movement was published in translation in Hungary.[3] György Gera (1922–1977), the Transylvanian-born (Nagyvárad/Oradea), Francophile poet,

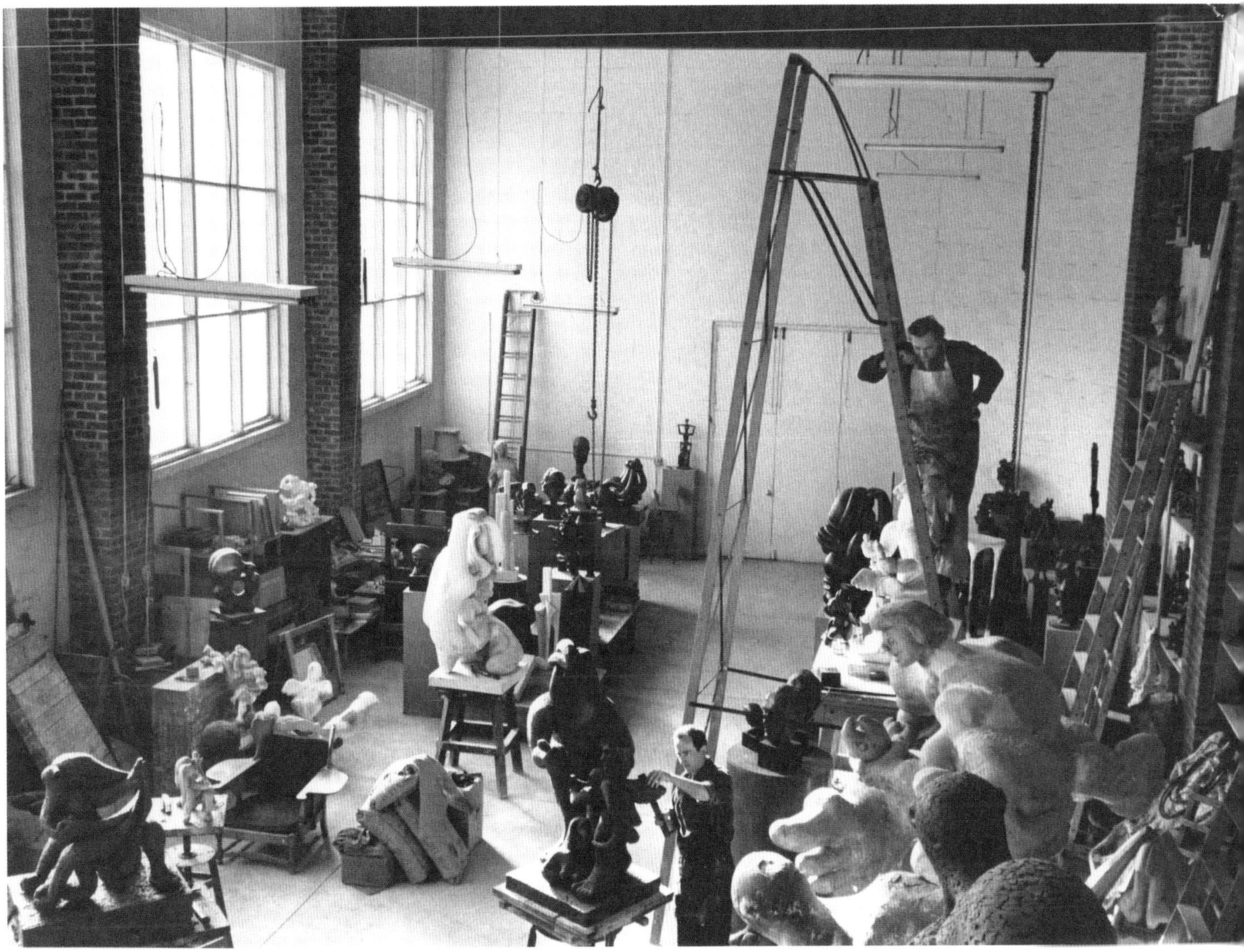

4 George Moffett, Jacques Lipchitz's studio at Hastings-on-Hudson, USA, ca. 1950
Musée d'art et d'histoire du Judaïsme, Paris, donation of Rubin Lipchitz

critic and editor who selected the extracts and pictures, wrote in the volume's introduction, "[Cubist] sculptors were comparatively better off. They had no need to transform the two-dimensional objects of the canvas into three dimensions, they were not overawed by the false alliance of perspective and illusion. At the same time, however, this delayed their realisation; their work was confined more solidly by material, more rigidly by anthropomorphism. Initially, moreover, they were subject to a kind of conditioned reflex. The fear that their autonomous art would lose its independence: that the paths of cubism would impoverish sculpture."[4]

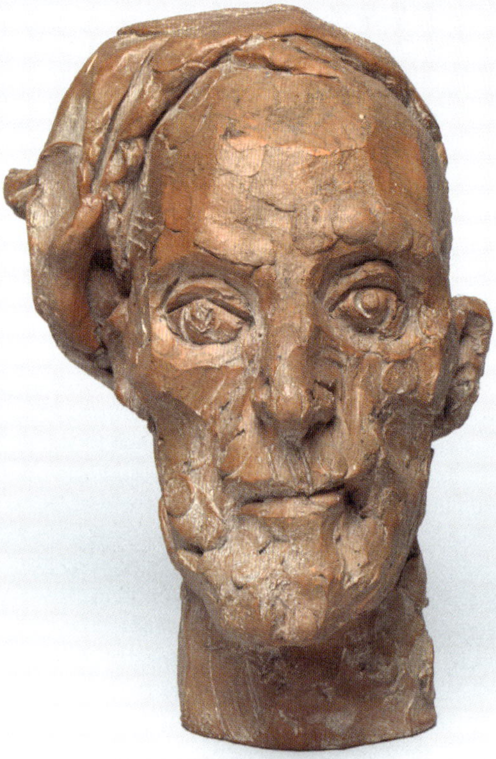

5a Jacques Lipchitz, *Géricault*, 1933
The Tate Gallery, London

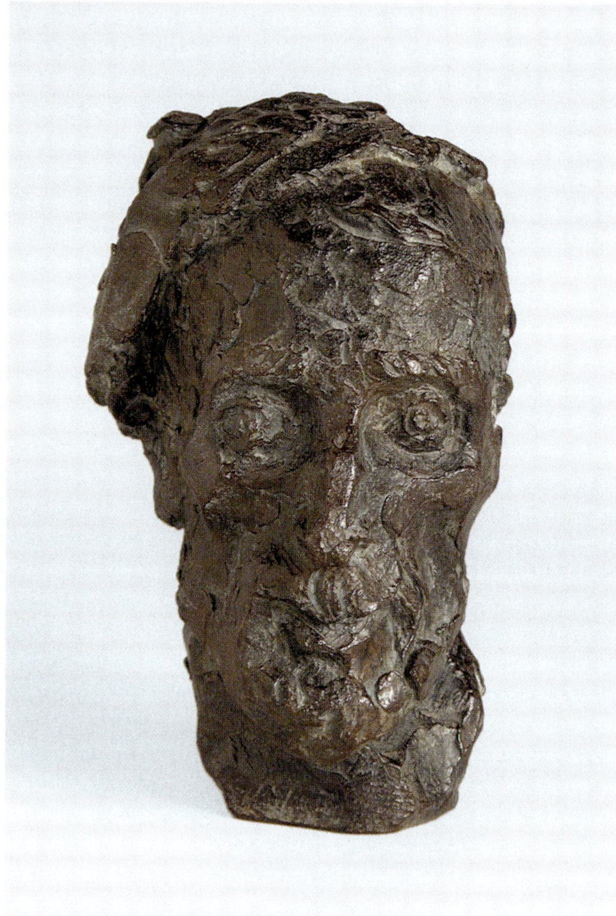

5b Jacques Lipchitz, *Géricault*, maquette no. 2, 1933
The Israel Museum, Jerusalem

The presentation of Lipchitz's sculptural œuvre was prepared for our volume by Dr Adina Kamien, senior curator and head of the department of Modern Art at The Israel Museum, Jerusalem. The items held in Budapest — six sculptures and two medallions, two drawings, prints, art books and documents, a few pieces from the artist's own collection, and a small fragment of his library — span a representative historical arc that begins with Lipchitz's cubist period and concludes with the bozzetti he made for his most important sculptures. It is of particular significance that these sculptures and bozzetti are being displayed in the museum where the Hungarian art historian Simon Meller (1875–1949), one of the greatest European experts on Renaissance small bronzes and models, once worked, collected, and conducted his scientific research, before tragically taking his own life in Paris in 1949.

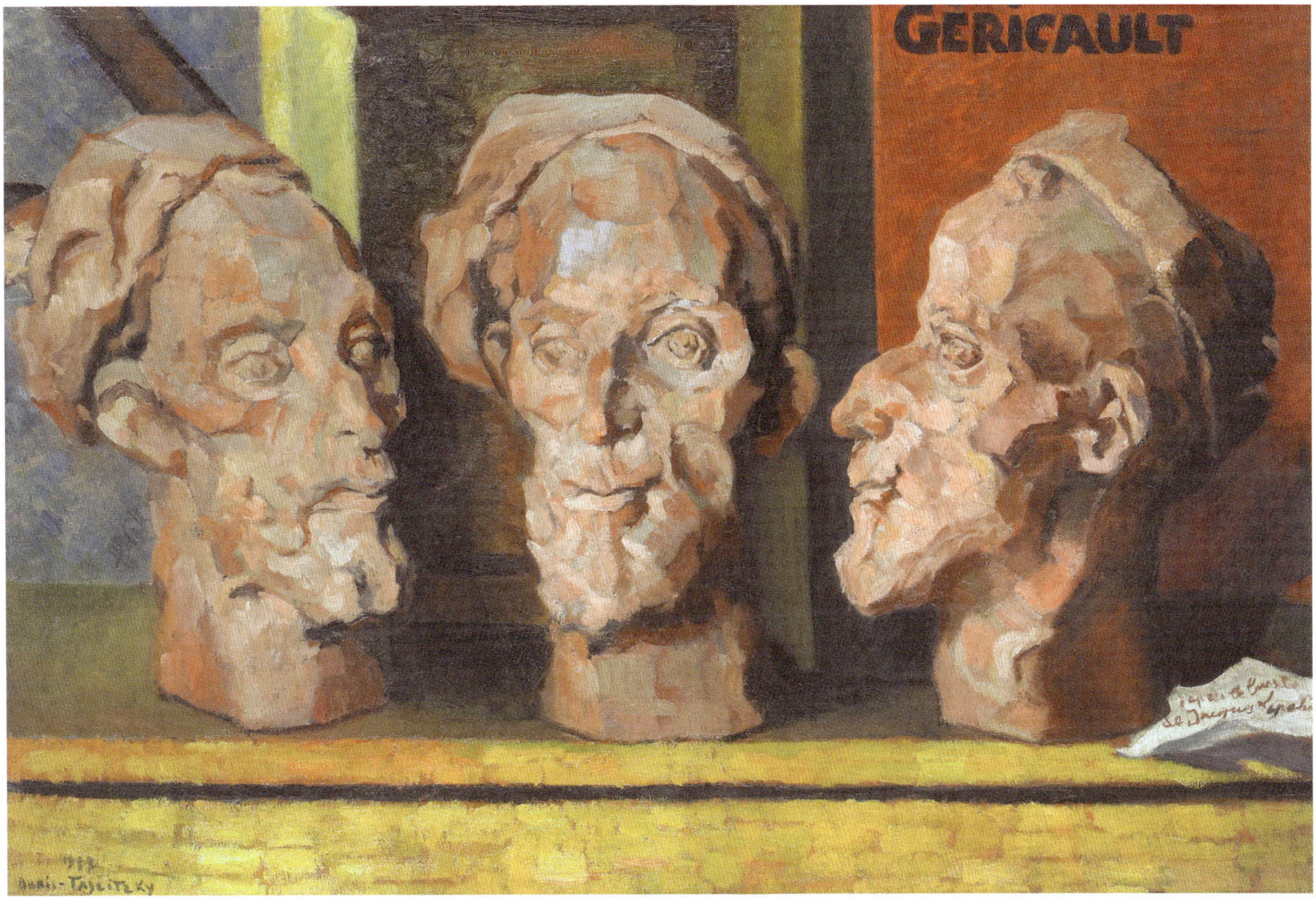

6 Boris Taslitzky, *Hommage to Théodore Géricault and Jacques Lipchitz*, 1937
Musée des beaux-arts de Rouen, Rouen

IN THE WAKE OF PAUL CEZANNE

Lipchitz's two cubist sculptures are truly remarkable pieces. The *Seated Pierrot*, cast in lead in 1922, was one of seven planned and executed versions. The one in Budapest was the third cast (cat. 1). Together with another work, a relief showing a female figure playing the guitar enclosed within a frame (cat. 2), the sculpture featured in the exhibition at the Museum of Fine Arts in 2021 entitled *Cezanne to Malevich. Arcadia to Abstraction*.[5] According to one of the main storylines of the commedia dell'arte, Pierrot pines for Columbine, his love for her unrequited. Distraught, he hunches over clutching his knees, staring into space. The melancholic motif, utilised several times by not only Lipchitz, but also his close friends Pablo Picasso (1881–1973) (fig. 7) and Juan Gris (1887–1927), echoes the paintings of

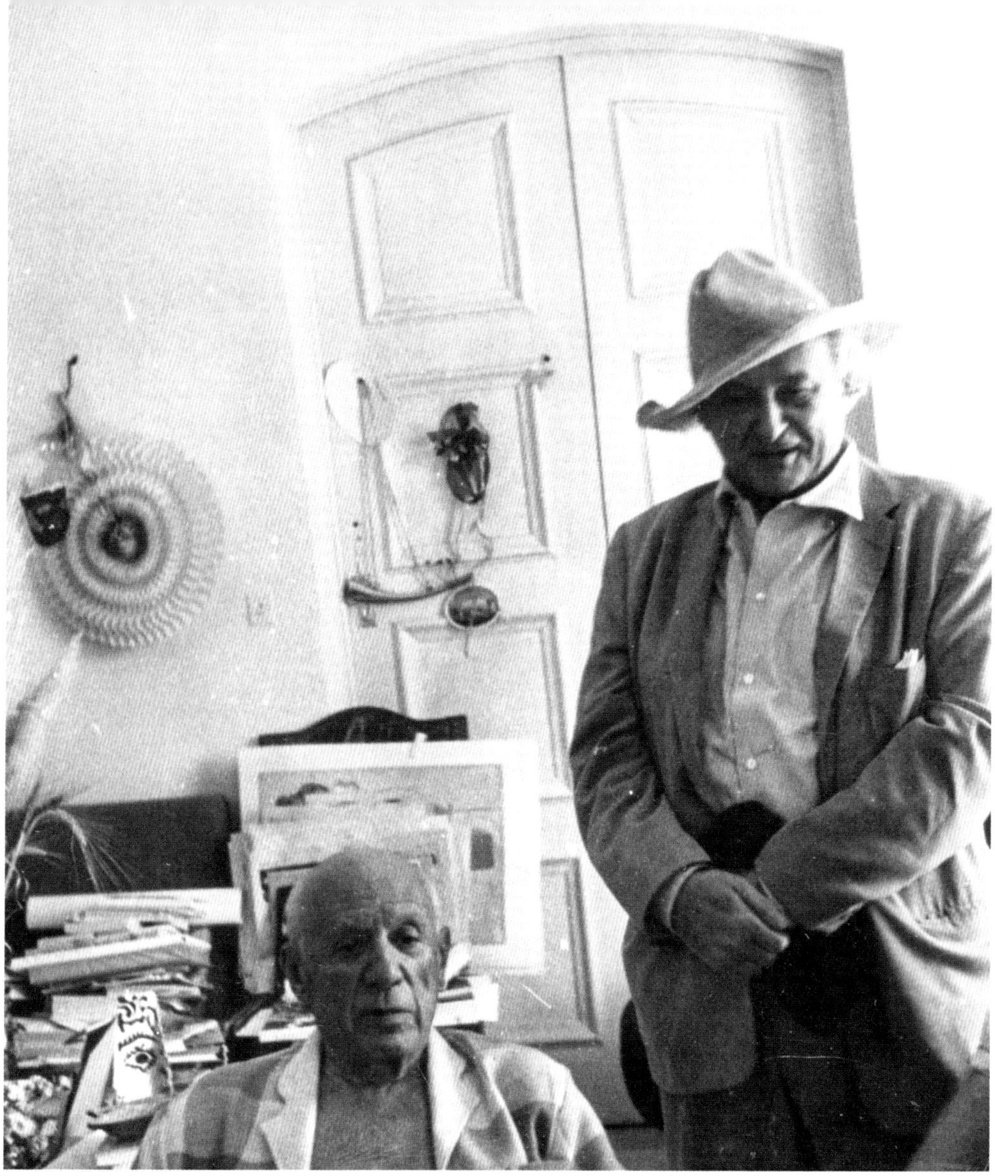

7 Jacques Lipchitz and Pablo Picasso in the South of France, ca. 1968
Private collection

Jean-Antione Watteau (1684–1721)[6] and several works by Paul Cezanne (1839–1906) from the late 1880s.[7] Lipchitz dismissed the idea that African primitive art had significantly prompted the emergence and development of cubism. While he and his fellows admired the works of primitive art in Paris's Museum of Ethnography, he claimed that "... the greatest source for cubism was unquestionably in the late works of Cézanne".[8]

On the relationship between the plane and the solid, Lipchitz thought similarly to his famous friend Picasso. They both emphasised the fruitful transition between different styles and movements, arguing that all schools of art followed the same principles and shared certain elements. Cubism was "an art dealing primarily with forms, and when a form is realized it is there to live its own life".[9] The two Budapest cubist sculptures by Lipchitz perfectly illustrate the central question of *The Cubism Seminars*, held in 2013 and 2014 in the Center for Advanced Study in the Visual Arts, Washington D.C.: What was Cubism? In his preface to the volume of lectures from the seminars, published in 2017, Harry Cooper, curator of Washington's National Gallery of Art, states quite plainly that, "Cubism, it should be said, is one of the worst names in the checkered history of modern *-isms*." He continues, however, "But what kind of art, if not an art of cubes?"[10] The experts at the seminars studied this question from all angles, examined the role of shade, the nature of brushwork in still lifes, the question of displacement,[11] the essence of cubism and silence, and other fundamental aspects. A thorough examination of the two *chefs d'œuvre* in Budapest can provide exhaustive answers to all these questions, and also to how the artist, arriving in Paris in 1909, became part of the fabric of the European avantgarde, and how he continued his work in the 1930s, for example by studying the paintings of Géricault.

Jacques Lipchitz — along with Pablo Picasso, Julio González (1876–1942), Constantin Brâncuşi (1876–1957), Alexander Archipenko (1887–1964) and Henri Laurens (1885–1954) — can be counted among the pioneering artists who proceeded in the wake of Paul Cezanne. Lipchitz was one of the innovators of twentieth-century sculpture. We would be mistaken, however, to imagine — as Herbert Read, the English art historian who is so popular in Hungary, asserted in his now somewhat outdated summary history of modern sculpture, published in 1964 — that sculptors at the start of the twentieth century owed little to artists from preceding eras. The sculptures of Jacques Lipchitz after 1930, or the works of, for example, Medardo Rosso (1858–1928), who has enjoyed a renaissance in the last twenty years, are also tied by multiple threads to the eighteenth- and nineteenth-century tradition.

In 1962 the English sculptor Reg Butler (1913–1981) published his lectures to his students, in which he summarised the fundamentals of sculpture. The aims he defined could easily serve to illustrate our present show as well as the modernist exhibition preceding it, entitled *Hantaï, Klee, and Other Abstractions*:[12] "The anatomical organization not merely of human beings but of animals, plants, bacteria, crystals, rocks, machines and buildings. The simplicity and complexity of their forms, their articulation, the disposition of stresses and strains in living and non-living structures. Recognition of the qualities of things; their hardness and softness, heaviness and lightness, tautness and slackness, smoothness and roughness.

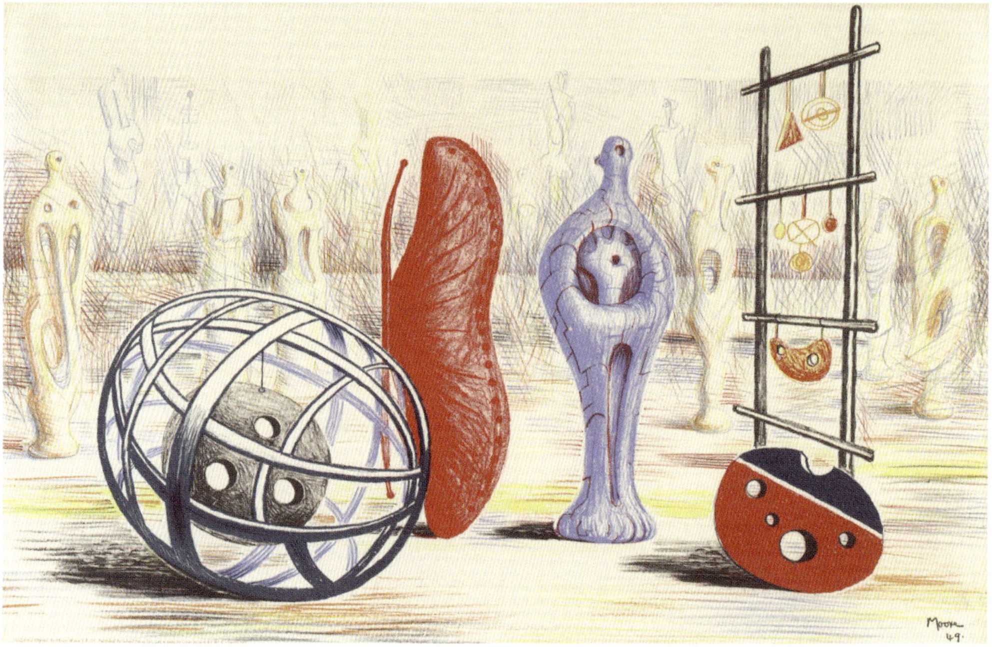

8 Henry Moore
Sculpture Designs, 1949
Museum of Fine Arts, Budapest

Recognition of unities and similarities, rhythms and analogues, differences. The character of space, the definition of space, the penetration of things into space. The nature of illumination, its determination of what we see ... The news value of colour. The way our reading of experience is controlled by the means by which we perceive."[13]

Lipchitz's *Reclining Nude with Guitar* of 1928 (Hirshhorn Museum and Sculpture Garden, Washington D.C., Tate Gallery, London, and The Museum of Modern Art, New York; cf. fig. 16) is considered a key work in the history of twentieth-century sculpture.[14] Some years earlier he had made the small Budapest bronze relief (cat. 2), which adheres more closely than the masterpiece entitled *Reclining Nude with Guitar* to cubist principles, about which Albert Gleizes (1881–1953) and Jean Metzinger (1883–1956) wrote in their treatise *On Cubism*, "The forms which are situated within [pictorial] space spring from a dynamism which we profess to dominate".[15] Compared with the tectonic and tranquil nature of his *Woman with a Guitar* (cat. 2), the *Reclining Nude with Guitar* has greater dynamism and alludes in essence to one of the basic questions in sculpture, namely to the enormous importance of the sculpture's interior space, the void, which later resulted in the unparalleled art of Henry Moore (1898–1986) (fig. 8) and Eduardo Chillida (1924–2002) (fig. 9). The latter both exerted a huge impact on the thinking of subsequent generations of sculptors by examining the relations between the form, the space inside the form, and the void.

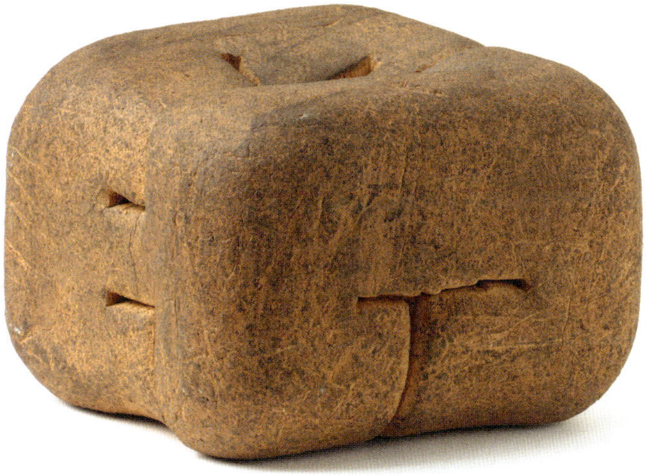

9 Eduardo Chillida
Lurra G-124, 1989
Museum of Fine Arts, Budapest

"THE PICTURE, ONCE LEFT, TORMENTS US AND PURSUES US" GÉRICAULT AND LIPCHITZ

By the end of the 1920s, the sculptural work of Jacques Lipchitz was imbued with everything that was later summed up by Herbert Read, as cited by Aniela Jaffé (1903–1991), a close associate of C. G. Jung: metaphysical anxiety characterises the whole of the modern world. Read also quoted Paul Klee (1879–1940), who wrote in his diary in 1915: "The more horrifying this world becomes … the more art becomes abstract …"[16]

In philosophy and in literature, the writings of Hippolyte Taine (1828–1893) and Marcel Proust (1871–1922) bring us close to the fleeting moments of our existence, but in the visual arts it is perhaps harder to trace and catch up with lost time. In sculpture, perhaps even more complexly than in painting, sensation and perception remain in motion. When Lipchitz moved on from his cubist period, his new works incorporated impressions from, inter alia, the most important sculptures of Auguste Rodin (1840–1917), such as *The Gates of Hell* (1890–1917). The surfaces of his sculptures become filled with signs and traces, sensitive almost to the point of becoming concrete physical experiences. Lipchitz's Budapest sculptures were made between 1922 and 1972, and it is as though they were following the aims defined by Reg Butler.

Margret Stuffmann, former director of the Department of Prints and Drawings at the Städel Museum in Frankfurt, in 2008 defined the three main leitmotifs driving the art of the great French romantic painter Eugène Delacroix as soul, imagination, and memory. The role of this trio of driving forces, especially that of memory, comes through quite naturally in the art of the impressionists, of the postimpressionist Cezanne, and of one of the main exponents of modern sculpture, Lipchitz. When we discovered in Jacques Lipchitz's library the publications on the entire œuvre of the other great romantic painter and Delacroix's contemporary, Théodore Géricault (fig. 10), we were immediately reminded of the words of Inken Freudenberg, Margret Stuffmann's outstanding pupil: "What we see before us [in our case here, at the birth of the cubist sculptor's new style, in the 1930s] never seems entirely new, but triggers an echo that is like a memory of 'every possible combination of shapes and forms' somehow already stored in our brain."[17] This notion, conceived of as early as the sixth century BCE, was referred to by Aleida and Jan Assmann as the "art of memory". The two eminent German researchers had a huge influence not only on our colleagues in Frankfurt, but thanks to their lectures in Budapest, also on Hungarian historians,

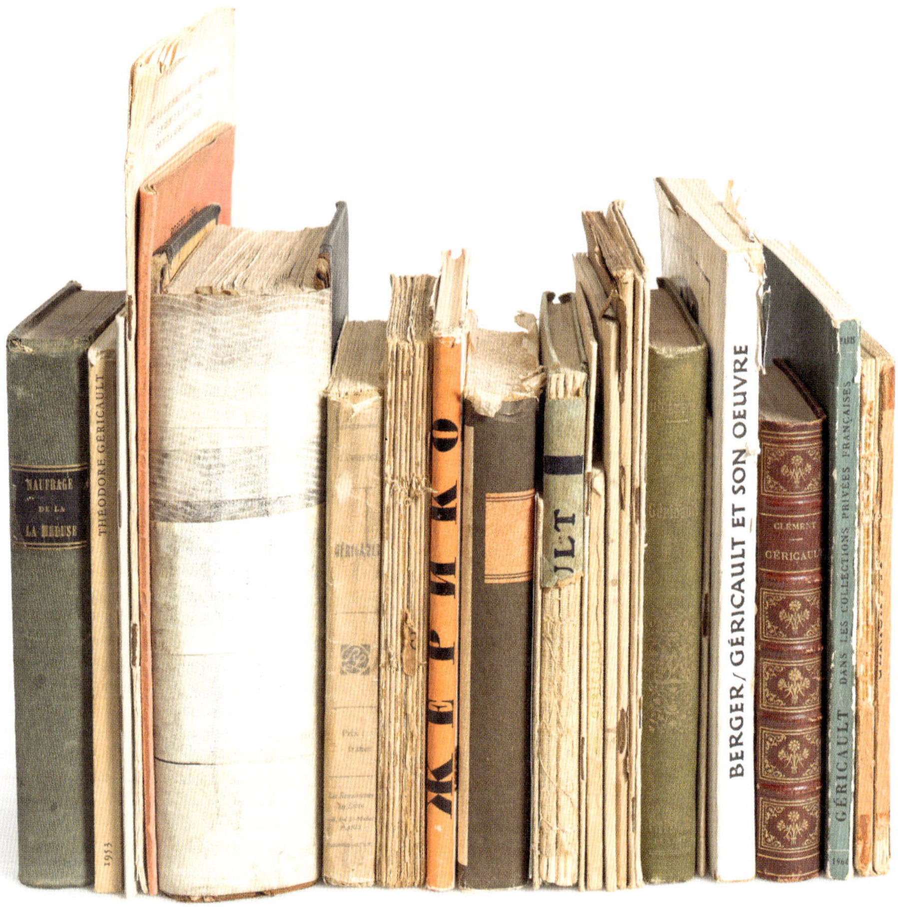

10 Books on Théodore Géricault in the library of Jacques Lipchitz

archaeologists, and art historians, and even writers and poets.[18] The painting and the sculpture, which proceeds above all from the memory, also speaks to the memory. In the course of 1855, Charles Baudelaire (1821–1867) and Théophile Gautier (1811–1872) intended this finding of theirs as a message to their contemporaries and to modernity.[19]

Some of the most beautiful and significant sculptures in our exhibition are the sketches made for *Our Tree of Life* (cats. 13–14), the study for *The Rape of Europa* (cat. 16), the aquatint *Theseus and the Minotaur* (cat. 7), and further major sculptures by Lipchitz may have been influenced by close study of the magnificent late paintings of Géricault. *The Start of the Barberi Race* (1817, Musée du Louvre, Paris)[20] and the wild, tumultuous composition of *Butchers of Rome (The Cattle Market)* (1817, Fogg Art Museum, Cambridge, Mass.)[21] stood at the centre of Lipchitz's interest, judging from the books and scholarly articles he collected over the decades and from the photographs in his collection.

What the viewer first perceives in Géricault's paintings is a dramatic commotion, the spectacle overpowering us before we have even grasped the theme; the same is true for Jacques Lipchitz's sculptures which were produced after the models in Budapest. The composition, the shading, the centripetal force conveyed in the centre: in much the same way, Paul Cezanne utilised the composition of Delacroix's 1827 painting *The Death of Sardanapalus* (Musée du Louvre, Paris) for his own *Pastoral* of 1870 (Musée d'Orsay, Paris), and then astonishingly applied this painterly solution to the compositional structure of certain still lifes.

AT REST IN JERUSALEM

The Metropolitan Museum of Art in New York organised a large-scale exhibition of Jacques Lipchitz's work not long before the artist's death. In parallel with this, in 1972 Lipchitz summarised his career in an autobiographical work titled *My Life in Sculpture*.[22] A few months later, at the age of eighty-two, Lipchitz passed away on the island of Capri.

At his request, he was buried in the city (fig. 11) where he had also deposited a significant part of his legacy. The Israel Museum in Jerusalem has been exemplary in the intervening decades at safeguarding and researching Lipchitz's legacy and collection. They pay full attention to the message of his heritage, a message which has happily also found its way to the Hungarian capital, Budapest.

Lipchitz's prophetic sculpture rests on the Jewish tradition, on Greek mythology, and on many elements of European culture. The Torah, however, proves to be an especially

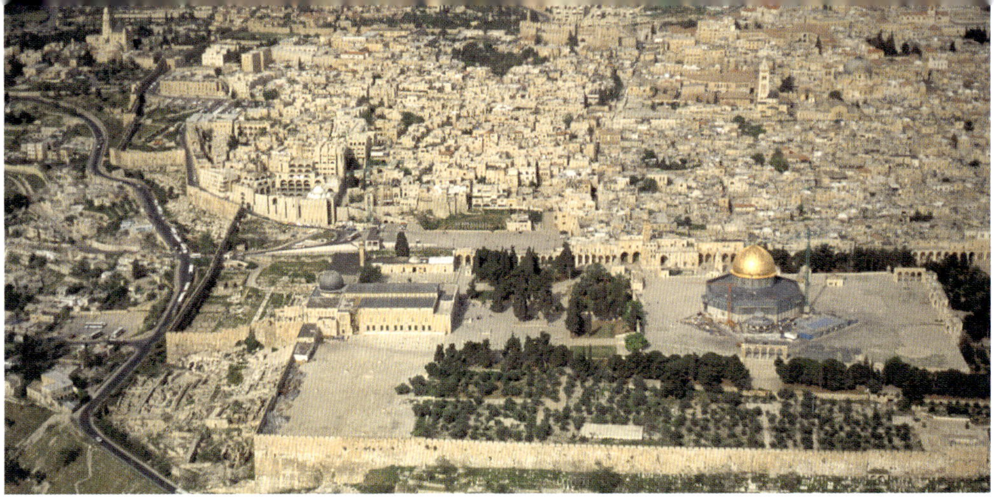

11 Jerusalem Old City, an aerial view of Temple Mount, 1995

powerful guide to understanding his life and his œuvre. "Because every generation interprets the Torah in accordance with their own needs, and in every generation God blesses the wise with keen eyes, that they may recognise in the Torah what is required for their age."[23] Gershom Scholem concluded, "The Jewish tradition does not establish systems of thought, but writes commentaries."[24]

Jacques Lipchitz did this through the expressive medium of sculpture, especially from the 1930s onwards. His work was commentary, visual commentary — as a spiritual attitude. He sculpted not what he saw, but what he thought.

NOTES

1 Pierre Reverdy, *La Réalité immobile*, from *La Lucarne ovale* (Paris: Briauld, 1916). English translation by Robert G. Cohn, in *Yale French Studies*, vol. 2, *Modern Poets* (Yale University Press, 1948). The poem also appears in Hungarian translation by Pál Justus in *Cubism* 1975 (see note 3), 232.
2 Similarly to other members of the family.
3 *A kubizmus. Válogatás a mozgalom dokumentumaiból* [Cubism. A selection of the movement's documents], ed. by András Székely, foreword, connective texts, excerpts, and illustrations selected by György Gera (Budapest: Gondolat Kiadó, 1975).
4 *Cubism* 1975, 34.
5 *Cezanne to Malevich. Arcadia to Abstraction*, exh. cat., ed. Judit Geskó (Budapest: Museum of Fine Arts, 2021).
6 Jean-Antoine Watteau, *Pierrot (Gilles)*, ca. 1718–1719, 184.5 × 149.5 cm, Musée du Louvre, Paris, inv.no. M.I.1121.
7 The entries on Jacques Lipchitz were written by Dimitri Ozerkov, see *Cezanne to Malevich* 2021, 316–19.
8 "Jacques Lipchitz. His Life in Sculpture," *The Metropolitan Museum of Art Bulletin* 30, no. 6 (June–July 1972): 286.
9 Pablo Picasso talking to Marius de Zayas: "Picasso Speaks," *The Arts*, New York (May 1923): 315–26; reprinted in Alfred Barr, *Picasso* (New York, 1946), 270–71. The text also appears in Hungarian translation by György Gellért in *Cubism* 1975 (see note 3), 152.
10 *The Cubism Seminars*, CASVA Seminar Papers 3, ed. Harry Cooper (Washington D.C.: National Gallery of Art, 2017), 1–2.
11 Judit Geskó, "The Structuralisation of Theme. Dóra Maurer and the Masters," in *Dóra Maurer. The Thematisation of Structure*, ed. Mónika Zsikla (Balatonfüred: Vaszary Gallery, 2024), 45–50.
12 *Hantaï, Klee, and Other Abstractions*, ed. and with an essay by Judit Geskó (Budapest: Museum of Fine Arts, 2022).
13 Reg Butler, *Creative Development: Five Lectures to Students* (Routledge & Kegan Paul, 1962), 58; cited in: Herbert Read, *Modern Sculpture* (London: Thames and Hudson, 1964), 215–17.
14 Abraham M. Hammacher, *Jacques Lipchitz* (New York: Harry N. Abrams, 1975), fig. 100.
15 Albert Gleizes and Jean Metzinger, *Du Cubisme* (Paris: Figuière, 1912); in English (translator unnamed) in: Robert L. Herbert (ed.), *Modern Artists on Art* (New Jersey: Prentice-Hall, 1964), 8.
16 Aniela Jaffé, "Symbolism in the Visual Arts," in C. G. Jung et al., *Man and His Symbols* (New York et al.: Anchor Press Doubleday, 1964), 265.
17 Inken Freudenberg, "'And the picture, once left, torments us and pursues us': Cézanne and Delacroix," in *Cézanne and the Past. Tradition and Creativity*, ed. Judit Geskó (Budapest: Museum of Fine Arts, 2012), 49–62, 498–99.
18 Cf. Jan Assmann, *Cultural Memory and Early Civilization: Writing, Remembrance, and Political Imagination* (Cambridge University Press, 2011). Originally published in German in 1992, first published in Hungarian in 1999.
19 Freudenberg 2012 (see note 17).
20 Lorenz E. A. Eitner, *Géricault. His Life and Work* (London: Orbis Publishing, 1983), 304, plate 23; Germain Bazin, *Théodore Géricault. Étude critique, documents et catalogue raisonné*, vol. 4, La bibliothèque des Arts (Paris: Wildenstein Institute, 1990), 202–3, no. 1368.
21 Ibid., 305, plate 24; Bazin 1990, no. 1219.
22 Jacques Lipchitz and Harvard H. Arnason, *My Life in Sculpture* (New York: The Viking Press, 1972).
23 Géza Komoróczy, "A kommentár mint szellemi magatartás és jelentősége a zsidó hagyományban" [Commentary as a spiritual attitude and its significance in the Jewish tradition], in Idem, *Történelem a próféták kezében. A Bibliáról* [History in the hands of the prophets. On the Bible] (Budapest: Ab Ovo Kiadó, 2019), 477. (First presented at the memorial session in honour of Chief Rabbi Sándor Scheiber, Budapest, 14 June 1988.)
24 Ibid.

MONOGRAPHIES, CATALOGUES, AND OFFPRINTS ABOUT THÉODORE GÉRICAULT (1791–1824) FROM THE FORMER LIBRARY OF JACQUES LIPCHITZ (GIFT OF RUBIN LIPCHITZ)

Corréard, Alexandre, and Jean-Baptiste Henri Savigny. *Relation du naufrage de la frégate la Méduse*. 4th edition. Paris: Palais-Royal, Galerie de Bois, 1821.

Clément, Charles. *Géricault. Étude biographique et critique avec le catalogue raisonné de l'œuvre du maitre*. Paris: Didier & Cie, 1868 (1st edition) / 1879 (3rd edition).

Rosenthal, Léon. *Géricault*. Paris: Librairie de l'art ancien et moderne, 1905. (2 copies)

J. Th. Géricault (1791–1824). Exhibition catalogue. Berlin: Fritz Gurlitt, 1907.

Géricault. Les Peintres illustres, 53. Paris: Pierre Lafitte et Cie, 1909.

Exposition d'œuvres de Géricault. Exhibition catalogue.
Paris: Hotel Jean Charpentier, 1924.

Régamey, Raymond. *Géricault*. Maîtres de l'art moderne.
Paris: F. Rieder & Cie, 1926.

Oprescu, George. *Géricault*. A Travers l'art français.
Paris: La Renaissance du Livre, 1927.

Exposition de dessins, aquarelles & gouaches par Géricault 1791–1824.
Exhibition catalogue. Paris: Maurice Gobin, 1935.

Gauthier, Maximilien. *Géricault*. Paris: Les Éditions Braun & Cie, 1935.

First Exhibition in America of Gericault. Paintings and Drawings. Exhibition catalogue. Introduction by Walter Pach. New York: Marie Sterner Galleries, 1936.

Géricault. Raconté par lui-même et par ses amis. Les Grands artistes racontés par eux-mêmes et par leurs amis. Edited by Pierre Courthion, Pierre Cailler. Vésenaz—Genève: Pierre Cailler, 1947.

Géricault, cet inconnu (1791–1824). Aquarelles, gouaches, dessins. Exhibition catalogue. Introduction by Waldemar-George. Paris: Galerie Bignou, 1950.

Berger, Klaus. *Géricault et son œuvre.* Translated by Maurice Beerblock. Paris: Bernard Grasset, 1952.

Invitation to the opening of the exhibition of Théodore Géricault, Kunstmuseum Winterthur, 20 August 1953.

Brochure of the exhibition of Théodore Géricault, Kunstmuseum Winterthur, 20 August to 8 November 1953.

Théodore Géricault. (1791–1824). Exhibition catalogue. Kunstmuseum Winterthur. Kunstverein Winterthur, 1953.

Gros, Géricault, Delacroix. Exhibition catalogue. Paris: J & H. Bernheim-Jeune, 1954.

Lebel, Robert. *Géricault. Ses ambitions monumentales et l'inspiration Italienne.* Paris: Robert Legueltel, 1962.

Žeriko o sebe i sovremenniki o nem [Géricault about himself and contemporaries about him]. Compiled, foreword, and notes by V. N. Prokofiev. Translated from French by T. A. Savitskaya. Moscow: Izdatelstvo Akademii Khudozhestv SSSR, 1962.

Géricault. Un réaliste romantique. Exhibition catalogue. Introduction by Olga Popovich and Robert Rousseau. Charleroi: Palais des beaux-arts, 1962–1963.

Exposition d'œuvres originales de Théodore Géricault (1791–1824). Peintures et dessins appartenant au Musée Bonnat. Exhibition catalogue. Introduction by Jean-Baptiste Lemoine. Bayonne: Musée Bonnat, 1964.

Marc Vaux
The wooden structure of Lipchitz's sculpture *Prometheus and the Vulture* (1937) in the artist's studio in Boulogne-sur-Seine
Private collection
›

Géricault dans les collections privées françaises. Exhibition catalogue. Introduction by Claude Roger-Marx. Paris: Galeire Claude Aubry, 1964.

Theodore Gericault (1791–1824) rajzai a roueni Szépművészeti Múzeum gyűjteményéből. [Drawings by Theodore Gericault (1791–1824) from the collection of the Museum of Fine Arts, Rouen]. Exhibition catalogue. Edited by Anna Szinyei Merse. Budapest: Magyar Nemzeti Galéria, 1982.

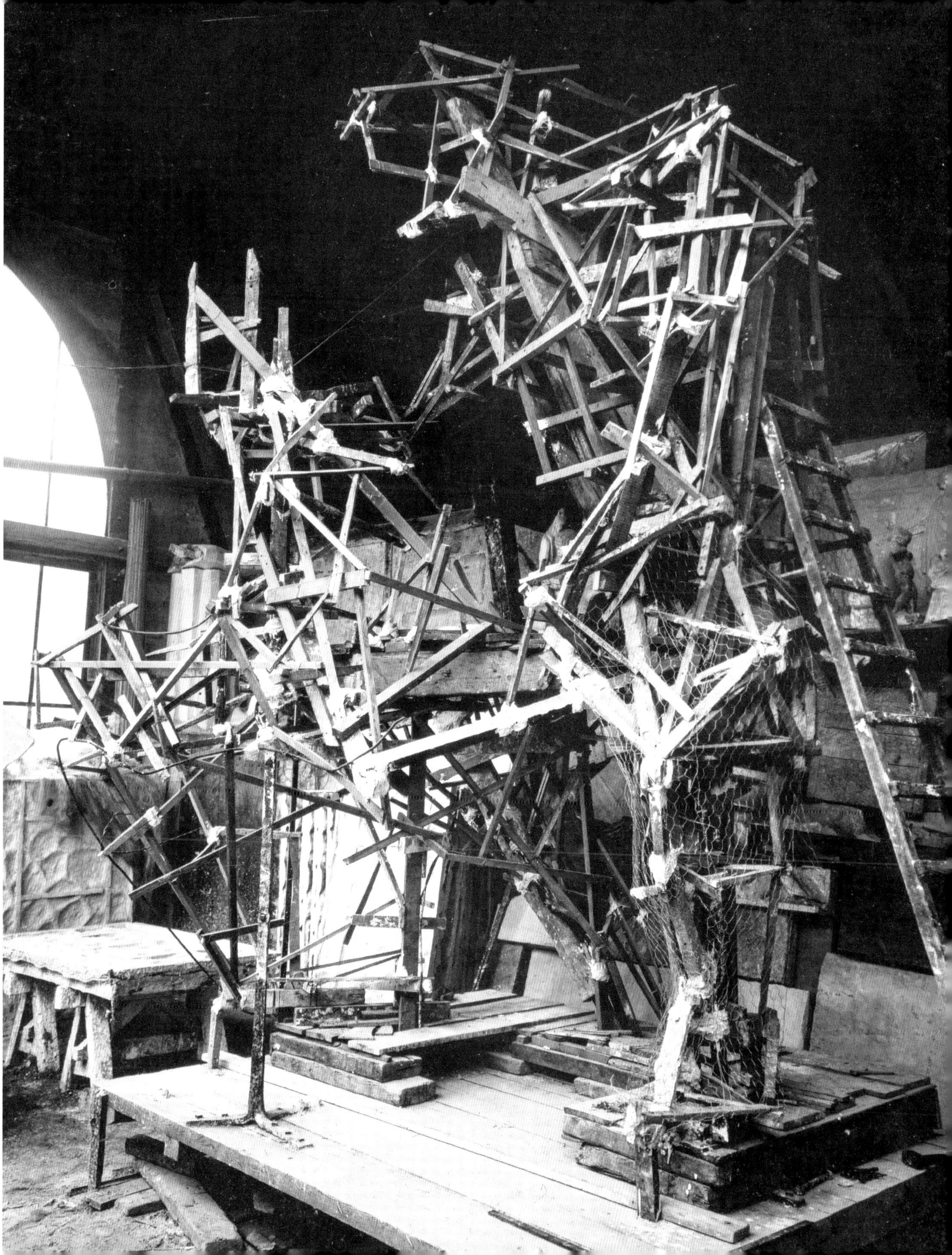

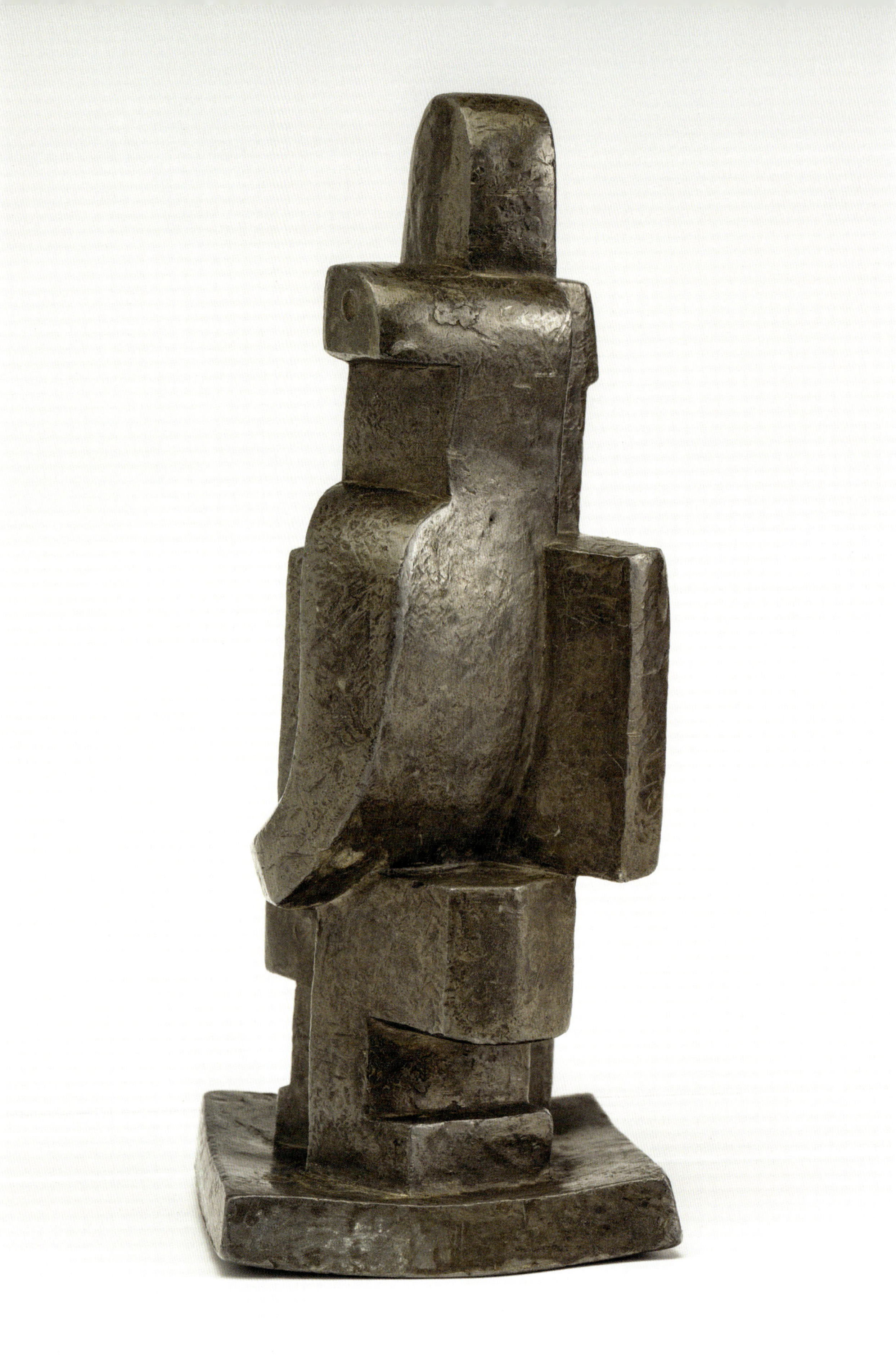

Adina Kamien

JACQUES LIPCHITZ: SCULPTURAL ENCOUNTERS

Cat. 1
Jacques Lipchitz
Seated Pierrot, 1922
Private collection
‹

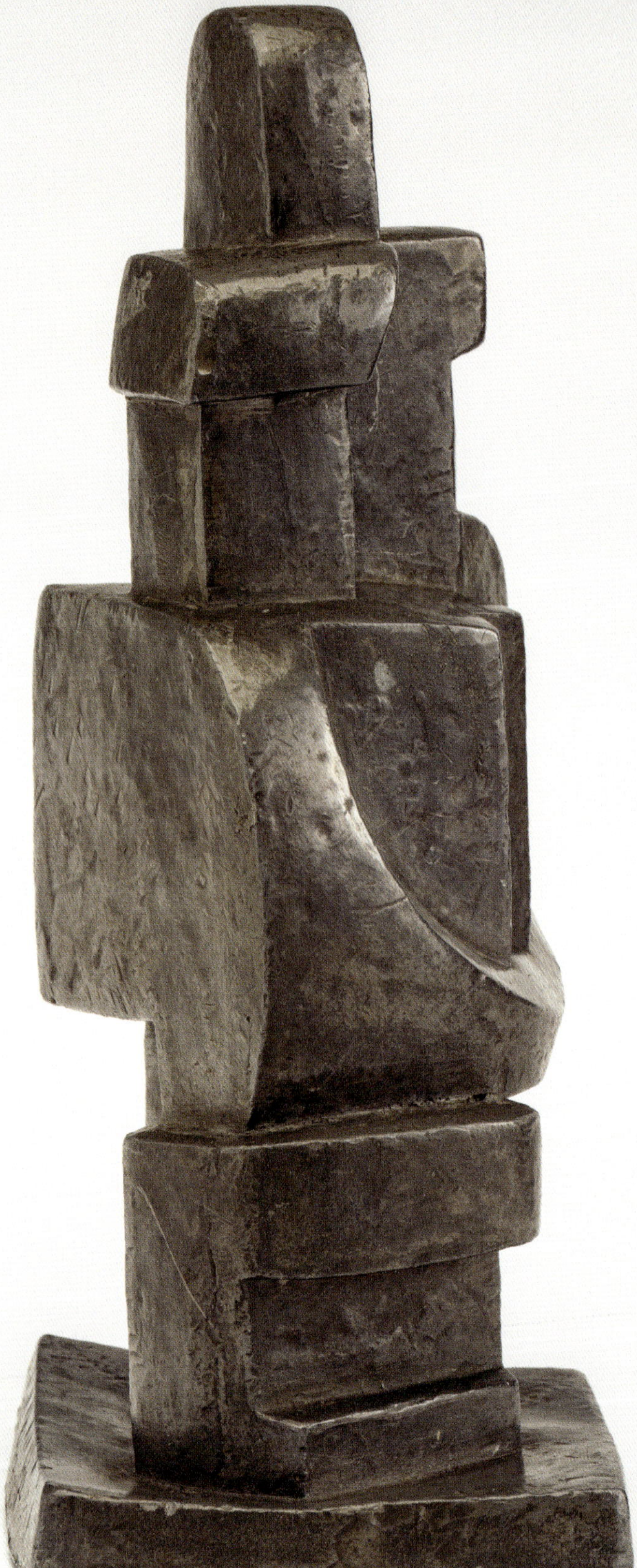

Jacques Lipchitz's creative output encompasses a wide range of subjects. He explored the human body, the theme of mother and child, encounters and struggles, mythological and biblical scenes, musical compositions, portraits, and monuments relating to war and peace. The private collection of Lipchitz's works on display at the Museum of Fine Arts' exhibition reflect moments of his long and fruitful sculptural œuvre, in a variety of materials and mediums: drawings and reliefs, bronze and lead sculptures.

Cat. 2
Jacques Lipchitz, *Woman with a Guitar*, detail, 1923–1924
Private collection

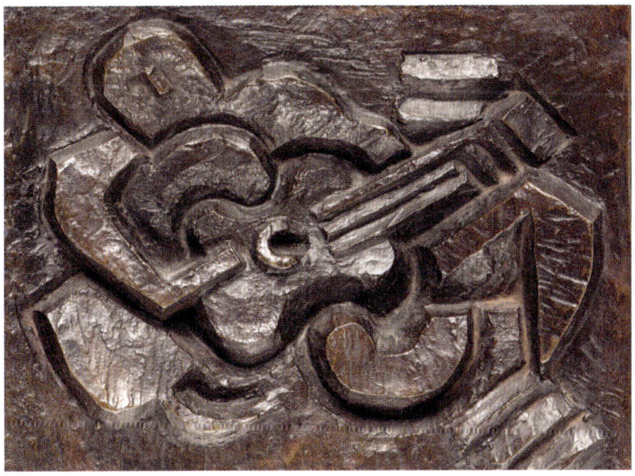

At the age of eighteen, in 1909, Lipchitz arrived in Paris from Lithuania. He met Pablo Picasso in 1913 through their mutual friend, Diego Rivera (1886–1957), and immediately understood the potential of cubism for his chosen medium — sculpture. The "syntax" of cubism liberated Lipchitz and helped him define his personality as an artist. Seeking a sculptural equivalent, between 1915 and 1925, cubism was, for Lipchitz, a means of re-examining sculpture as a three-dimensional art in space, mass, plane, and line (cats. 1–2). Lipchitz felt that "... cubist sculpture, by the very three dimensional nature of the sculpture medium, contributed importantly to the cubist definition of space in painting".[1] According to art historian H. Harvard Arnason, who published *My Life in Sculpture* with the sculptor in 1972, "the cubist sense of form has remained with Lipchitz throughout his life, even though his style has departed radically from that of cubism".[2]

Seated Pierrot (cat. 1) is a rigidly vertical figure, which despite its frontality, exudes a great sense of three-dimensionality. An important development in Lipchitz's work is the way in which he creates volume through receding voids between the planes. The head and body are constructed of varied flat planes placed at right angles to one

Cat. 1
Jacques Lipchitz
Seated Pierrot, 1922
Private collection

another in a cruciform shape. The upper and lower parts are linked by a horizontal, circular plane. Lipchitz clarified the differences in mediums: "I made a colored drawing of a Pierrot about the same time that is closely related to this sculpture, but if the two are compared, the difference between cubist painting and cubist sculpture becomes clear. In the drawing, which is, of course, organized on a flat surface, the planes are tilted at angles to the surface to create a limited sense of depth from the plane of the picture that reinforces that plane. In the free-standing sculpture it was necessary to emphasize the three-dimensional quality; and for this reason I organized the planes at right angles to one another. This is a kind of bone structure that exists firmly in space like a skeleton."[3] His aim was to create, "... balance between the nonfigurative form and figuration for which I was unconsciously seeking".[4]

Still life elements such as clarinets, guitars, and other musical instruments appear frequently in cubist paintings of Picasso, Georges Braque (1882–1963), and Gris. In Lipchitz's work, figures and musical instruments become abstract shapes, an integrated puzzle in which interlocking pieces fit together to create a kind of melodic harmony.[5] In 1922, Dr Albert C. Barnes commissioned Lipchitz to create seven bas-reliefs and two sculptures for the exterior of his house and art gallery at Merion, Philadelphia. For this commission Lipchitz returned to his earlier cubist reliefs of musical instruments of 1917–1918. "... in the reliefs I did for Barnes and particularly in the preliminary maquettes for these reliefs ... I was intrigued by a contrast of opposites, the highly organic, freely flowing figure-form set within a rigidly geometric architectural frame. In other reliefs ... such as the lunette for Barnes, the entire figure composition is so free that it can be described as baroque in its movement."[6]

During 1923 and 1924 he made a number of small relief sculptures as studies. In *Woman with a Guitar* (cat. 2), we see Lipchitz integrating the human figure with the instruments. "The subject is a reclining figure with a guitar," he wrote of a related work, "the curved shape of the right leg is also the shape of the guitar. This is again a total assimilation of the figure to the guitar-object; even the left arm reiterates the shape of the guitar. The work is massively conceived in curvilinear volumes, with a strong sense of frontality, but involving a movement in and out of depth. Thus, the lower, or right, leg is composed at a diagonal directing the eye through the space below the left leg. Similar planar diagonals under the head and the left arm emphasize the opening void."[7] *Woman with a Guitar*, in relatively high relief, treats the subject with great freedom of movement. Lipchitz deepened the surfaces, the objects having light curves creating shadow. The curvilinear cubism reveals the artist's desire in the early 1920s to escape the constrictions of literal cubism.

After a decade of groundbreaking work in the cubist idiom, Lipchitz's style changed, and from the late 1920s, the earlier emphasis on form and structure gave way to the expression of emotional states through elasticity and movement. From 1925 onwards, wax modelling and bronze casting became Lipchitz's preferred techniques. The sculptures become more dynamic, rhythmic structures of growth.

With the rise of fascism in Nazi Germany in 1933, Lipchitz turned to social and political expression; his works embody dualistic themes: battles between people, between man and animal, and symbols of good and evil forces in life. Following Lipchitz's escape to the United States in 1941, he synthesised themes of earlier periods and developed a deep interest in the mysteries of rebirth and regeneration.

Lipchitz's left-wing leanings led him to take an interest in the Soviet Union. He was impressed with the ideals and achievements of the Russian Revolution and accepted a proposal to make a monument entitled *Towards a New World* for which *maquette no. 4* (cat. 5) is a study. In 1935, he visited his family in the Soviet Union, with his first designs for the monument. In order to express the "liberation of the Russian people through industry and agriculture," he envisaged a column topped by dancing figures. Ultimately, his project was not accepted.

Cat. 5
Jacques Lipchitz
Towards a New World,
maquette no. 4, 1934
Private collection

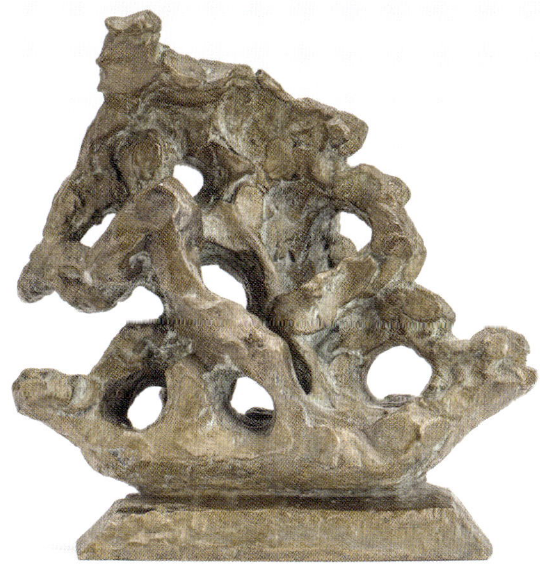

After the war, he revisited the composition as a starting point for a commission for a large public sculpture entitled *The Spirit of Enterprise* received in 1950 from the Fairmount Park Art Association in Philadelphia — his first commission for a major public sculpture since arriving in America from Paris in 1941. The work was to capture "The physical power of men, their imaginative dreams, the surge of their material expansion, the skill of craftsmanship, the power of labor."[8] The finished sculpture, an allegorical figure over four meters wide, stands in the central terrace of the Ellen Phillips Samuel Memorial Sculpture Garden in Philadelphia. According to the artist: "Most of the surviving maquettes of 1934 and 1935 are projects for monuments. Aside from the *David and Goliath* and the Soviet Monument, I made the initial designs entitled *Towards a New World*, which I was finally able to complete as *Enterprise* for Fairmount Park in Philadelphia, in the 1950s."[9] The four surviving maquettes show figures carrying a flag. Shaped in a pyramidal form, roughly modelled figures interpenetrate spatially. A great undulating flag sweeps over, encompassing the group. "*Toward a New World* was also

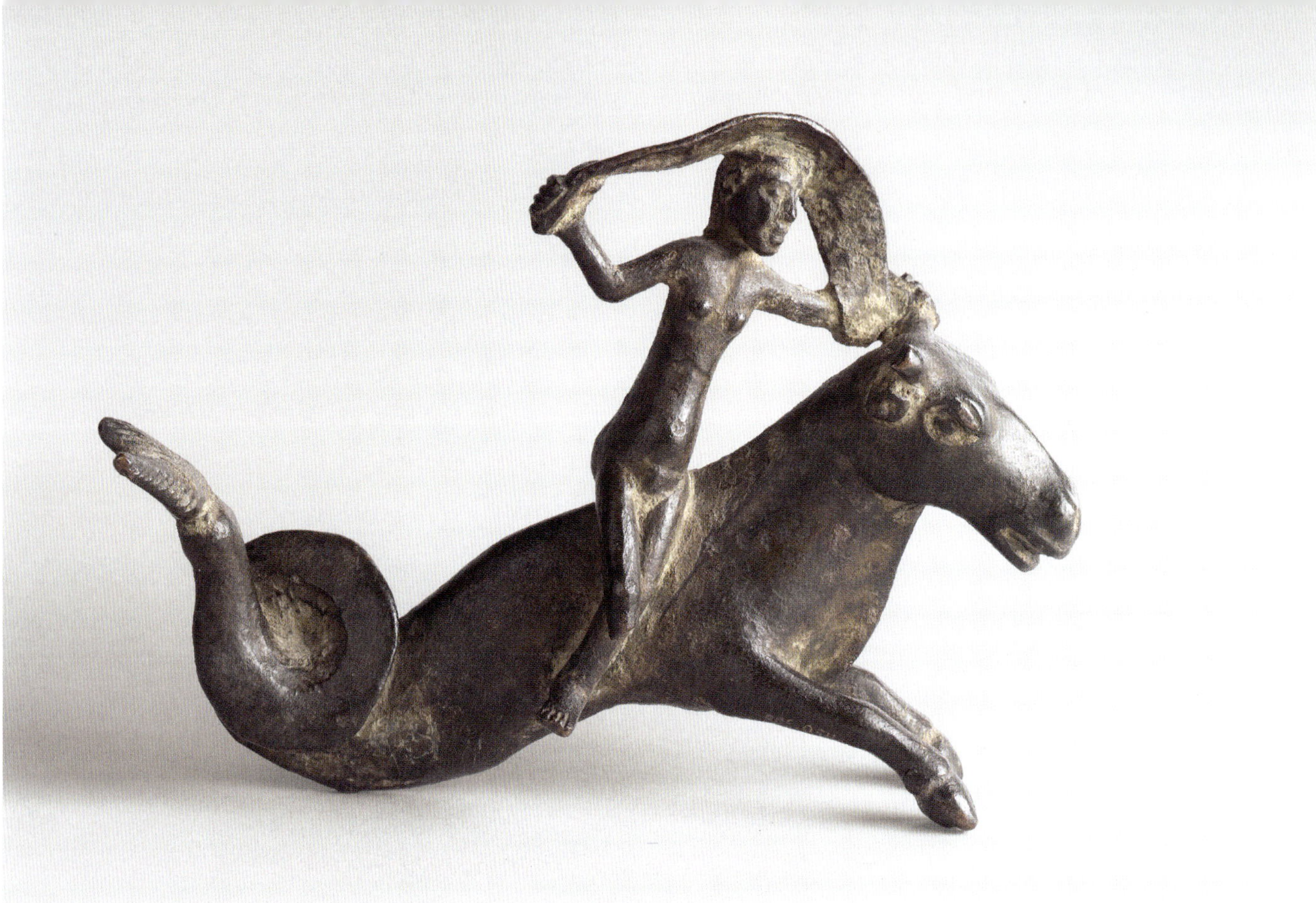

12 Statuette of Nereid
Riding a Sea Monster
Egypt, Coptic (?), 4th–5th centuries
The Israel Museum, Jerusalem

one of the very few political sculptures I have made, suggestive of my momentary enthusiasm for the revolutionary cause of Russia, an enthusiasm which did not survive very long, because I have always been and continued to be on the side of freedom and against any form of oppression or dictatorship."[10]

Lipchitz took up the subject of *The Rape of Europa* at first in 1938, making three small sculptures. In this sketch (cat. 16), the dynamic group emphases volume and texture, composed as a series of rises, falls, and protrusions. The pointy horned bull grabs the woman by her fleshy thigh as her arms flail in the air. The multi toned brown patina gives the work an earthy, sensual feel. The theme derived from Lipchitz's personal associations and increasing interest in classic myth: "All of my sculpture derives from something in my life, a desire or a dream. In the bull who carries off Europa and swims with her to Crete, the appendages at the back suggest a fishlike form. In my collection there is an extremely rare bronze Coptic piece in which the bull takes on different aquatic shapes (fig. 12). I think that I may have been influenced by this. The general forms of the bull and Europa probably derive from the earlier bull and condor, although, as is so frequently the case with my sculpture, the conflict and terror of the earlier version is here transformed into erotic love."[11]

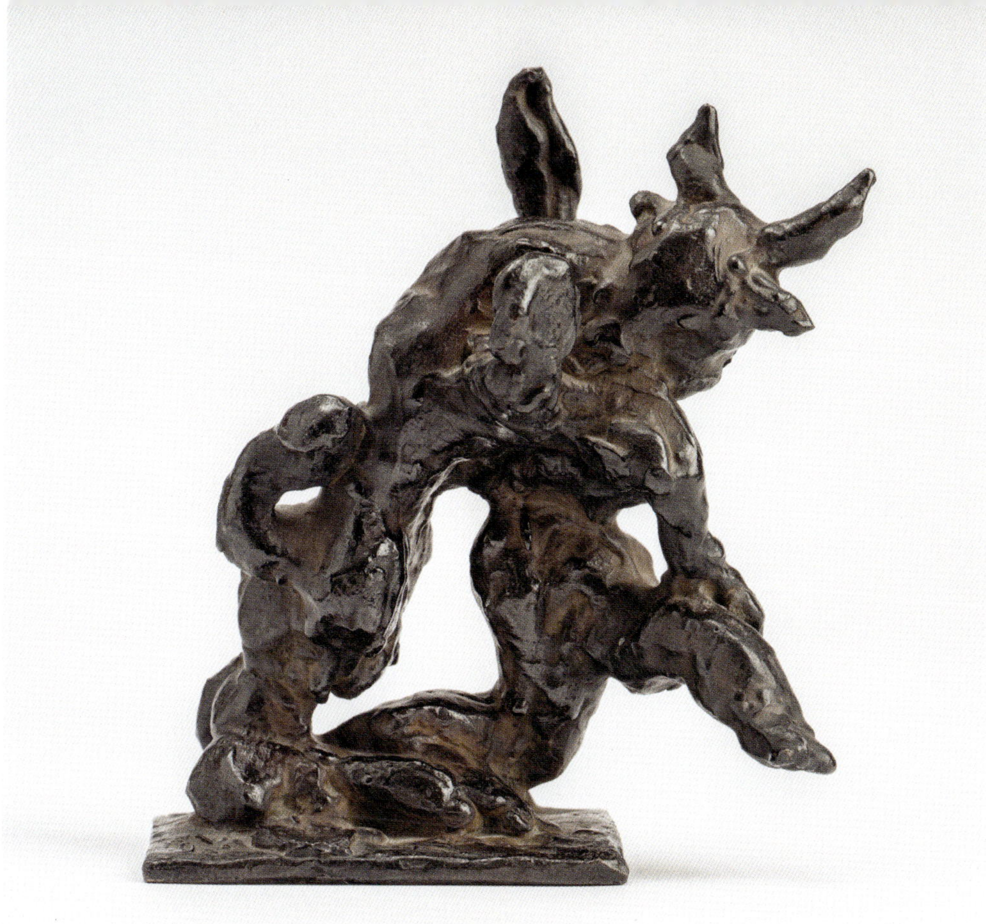

Cat. 16
Jacques Lipchitz
Small study for *The Rape of Europa*, 1969–1970
Private collection

Lipchitz took up the subject of *The Rape of Europa* again in America in 1941. He transformed the dynamics in the second version: "I used the theme of the *Rape of Europa* later in a quite different context, the Europa as a symbol for Europe and the bull as Hitler, with Europe killing Hitler with a dagger. This reverses the concept to one of terror, whereas in the original sculptures of Europa the entire theme is tender and erotic love; the bull is caressing Europa with his tongue."[12] Arnason underlines that "the idea of change or becoming goes like a thread through the sculpture of Lipchitz. In it are involved all the thoughts that the artist has had on birth and life and death. Europa, assimilated to the bull, becomes one with the godhead. Theseus killing the Minotaur seems to be destroying a part of himself."[13]

This Coptic piece to which Lipchitz referred was one of thousands of artefacts he accumulated, from Africa and Oceania, the Americas and Asia, medieval Europe and the ancient world. His captivating collection, containing some three thousand objects from cultures whose motifs, techniques, and ways of expression enriched and influenced Lipchitz's own creativity, was gifted to The Israel Museum by the Lipchitz Family. "My collection of objects from all periods in history is of immense importance to me, even if some of the pieces in it are not so important, so significant in themselves; but it is like a university to me. I have learned something from every work, something that has helped me to understand certain things about sculpture in general and about my own sculpture in particular. It is a sculptor's collection, and this is why I hope it can be kept together. I think that future generations of artists and art students can learn about themselves and their own work by studying it. When I speak of my learning from the collection, I do not, of course, mean taking subjects or even motifs. Rather, what I have learned by constantly handling these objects and looking at them, living with them, are such things as forms, techniques, the ways in which an ancient or primitive sculptor-artist approached his materials. For instance, I am continually fascinated by the ways that ancient and primitive peoples experimented with bronze; how frequently daring and imaginative they could be in their handling of the material, much more so than many bronze sculptors of Renaissance and modern times."[14]

13 "Cabinet of Curiosities", on display at the Jacques Lipchitz Collection in The Israel Museum, Jerusalem
Gift of the Lipchitz Family
›

The collection reflects a fascination with human imagination and artisanship, exemplifying what he called "encounters": similarities among objects made in very different periods and places. The collection evokes the "Wunderkammer" of the past — eclectic cabinets of curiosities filled with objects from cultures of all kinds (fig. 13). This collection also gives us a glimpse into the artist's actual studio, allowing us to share (in some measure) what Lipchitz himself experienced: "I look at all that surrounds me, and feel the whole of humanity with me. I am never alone, never lost, and given, with a sense of humility, the courage for my every day's work."[15]

Lipchitz derived inspiration from his Jewish heritage, and frequently chose themes connected with the Bible, Jewish life and history. He was invited to Israel for the first time in the autumn of 1962, together with his wife Yulla and daughter Lolya, spending three weeks traveling around the country with Karl Katz, then director of The Israel Museum. Lipchitz met with Teddy Kollek, Jerusalem's visionary mayor and future founder of The Israel Museum, and had breakfast with Prime Minister David Ben-Gurion. The sculptor created several works that relate directly to Israel.[16] In 1967, Lipchitz was commissioned by Mayor Teddy Kollek to create a Commemoration Medal on the Unification of Jerusalem, which upon completion was presented to the State of Israel. Lipchitz next came to Israel in 1971 for his retrospective exhibition on the occasion of the inauguration of the Tel Aviv Museum of Art. In Jerusalem, The Israel Museum presented an exhibition in honour of the artist's 80th birthday, celebrating the donation of a large collection of bronze sketches from the sculptor's brother, Rubin Lipchitz.

›
Cat. 13
Jacques Lipchitz
Sketch for *Our Tree of Life*, version II, 1971–1972
Private collection

Having worked on a massive sculpture of the Virgin Mary in France, in 1962 Lipchitz decided to create a monument to the development of Judaism — *Our Tree of Life*,

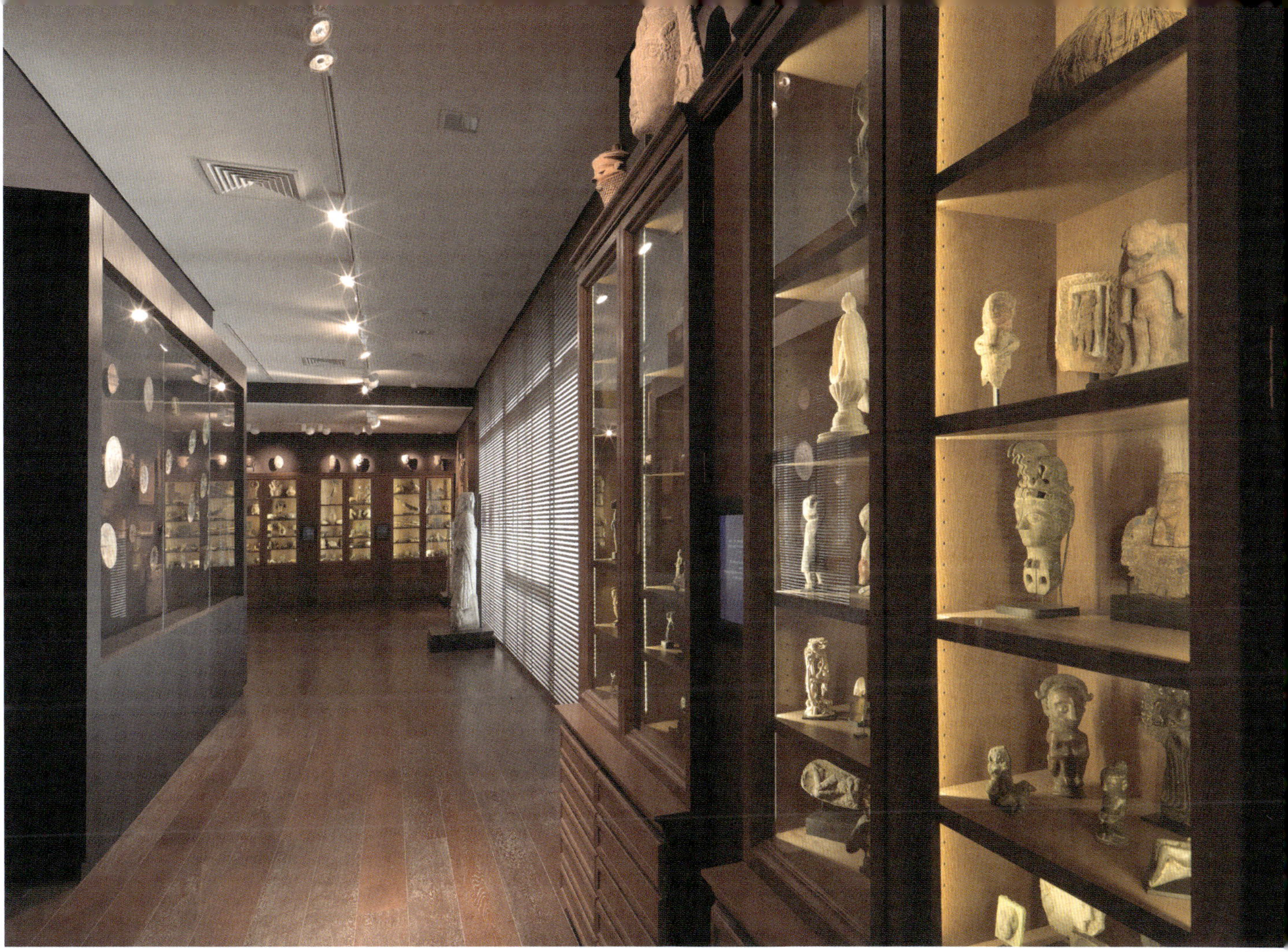

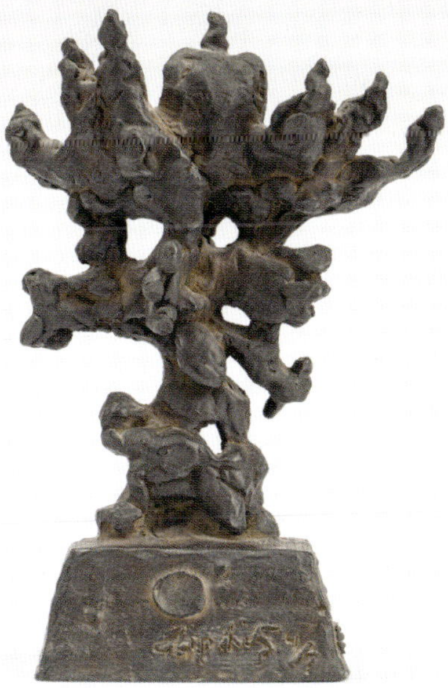

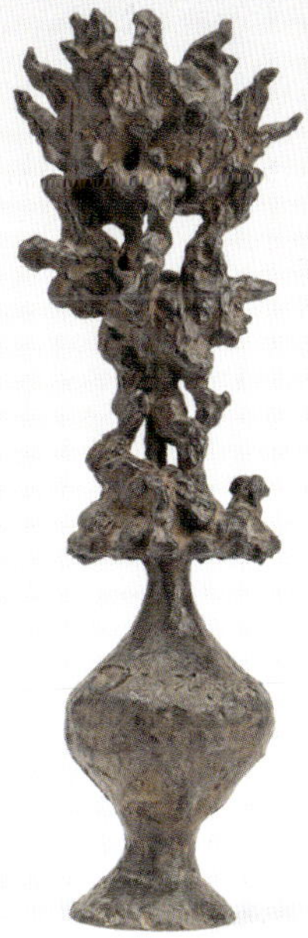

Cat. 14
Jacques Lipchitz
Sketch for *Our Tree of Life*,
version IV, 1971–1972
Private collection

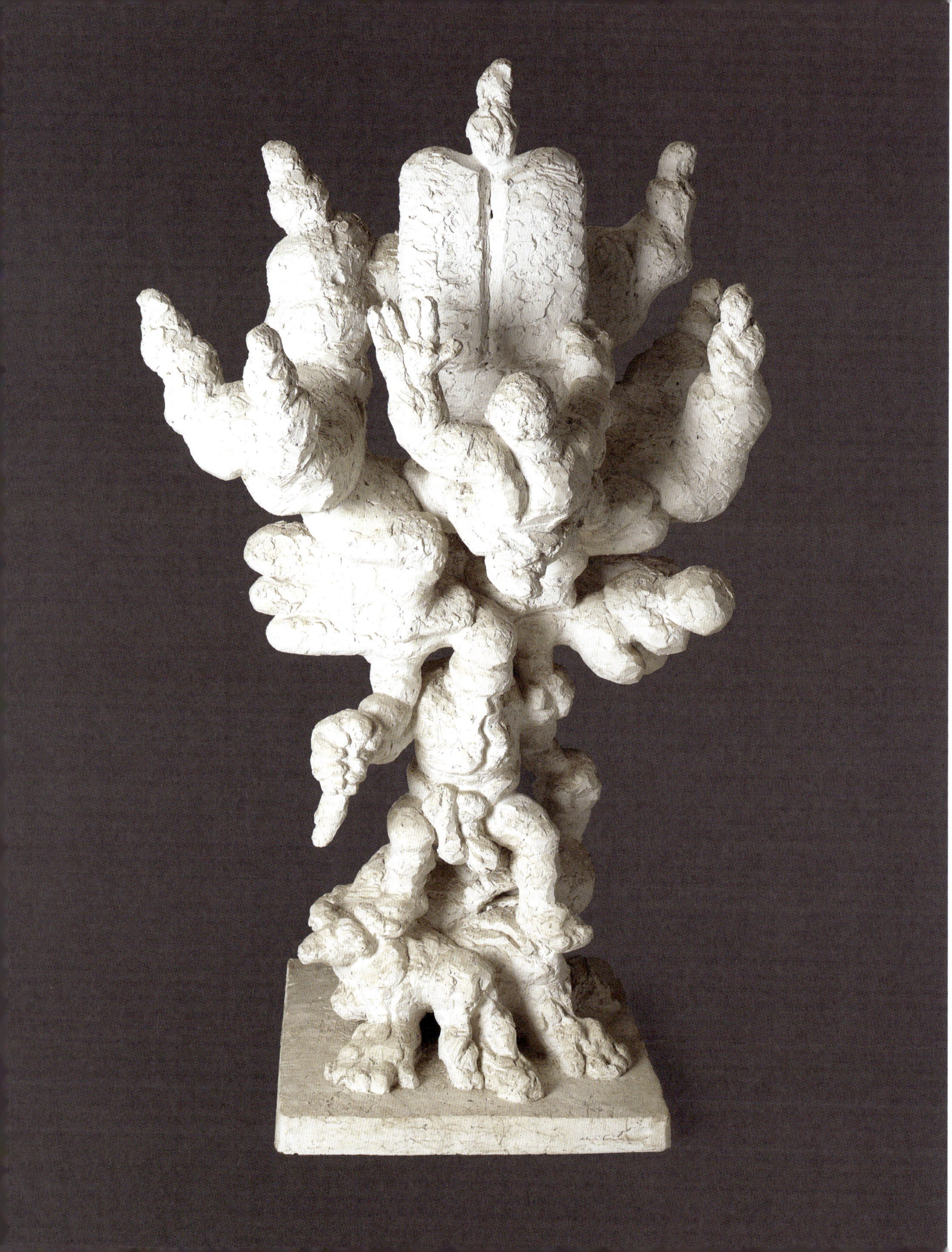

representing the Jewish patriarchs, the burning bush and the tablets of the law. The flame, a symbol of metamorphosis and purification, became the basic form and concept of *Our Tree of Life*. This project yielded multiple versions and sketches (cats. 13–14).

14 Jacques Lipchitz, final sketch for *Our Tree of Life*, 1973
The Israel Museum, Jerusalem
Gift of the Jacques and Yulla Lipchitz Foundation, Inc.

In one version Abraham appears at the base, surmounted by the three Patriarchs. Moses surrounded by the burning bush forms the upper part, with a phoenix rising above. In his later works Lipchitz often stacked interrelated elements. He isolates Abraham as the physical and conceptual "trunk" of the tree, depicted at the moment in which the angel prevents him from sacrificing Isaac.

During the 1971 visit, Lipchitz chose Hadassah University Hospital on Mount Scopus as the site for his sculpture *Our Tree of Life*. In 1973 Lipchitz completed the definitive maquette (fig. 14), and the six-meter-high bronze was unveiled posthumously in 1978. The sculpture depicts Noah, the Sacrifice of Isaac with the angel restraining Abraham, Moses in front of the Burning Bush, and rising above—a phoenix supporting the Two Tablets.[17] The form of *Our Tree of Life* reminds of the flame, "the supreme symbol of metamorphosis and purification".[18]

In his autobiographical *My Life in Sculpture,* Lipchitz recounted: "Now I am making *Our Tree of Life* as a monument for Israel, and I have been rethinking the problem. I have decided to start not with Abraham but with Noah, who is the actual patriarch of the Jews, the father of the Jewish people. Everything builds on the figure of Noah. *Our Tree of Life* is still in process. I have not yet arrived at a satisfactory solution. There is a large sketch in my studio that I have been working on for six or seven years that is constantly changing. Even this year I made major changes. I hope that soon I can find the final image."[19]

Lipchitz saw his sculptural projects as expressions of his human development: "There are several sketches for the Israel monument but none of them is final. I am still trying to develop my ideas. I am still, like my father, putting one brick after another in the building of a house, attempting to make a final statement. I would like to be able to make this at the end of my life, or, as my father always said, to come to the roof."[20]

During his 1971 visit to Israel, Lipchitz travelled to Kfar Chabad to celebrate his upcoming birthday. He toured the small village with his wife Yulla and her son Hanno Mott, and Lipchitz recalled his childhood and memories of Chassidic dance, which invigorated his work.[21] Fulfilling his request to be buried by Chabad in Jerusalem, following his death on 26 May 1973 on the island of Capri, Lipchitz was buried on

15 Jacques Lipchitz *The Struggle*, 1973 The Israel Museum, Jerusalem
›

Har Hamenuhot in Jerusalem. Shortly before his death Lipchitz created a model for a silver salver, commemorating the 25th anniversary of the State of Israel. He chose as his subject the image of Prometheus locked in fierce battle with a giant vulture, holding a menorah high over his head. This symbolised for Lipchitz the triumph of light over darkness, education over ignorance, and the struggle for Jewish survival and liberation (fig. 15). In the Budapest *Medallion with Self-Portrait* (cats. 18–19), a simplified athletic figure wielding what looks like a forge (the artist as a young man?) appears on one side of the plaque, while on the other a dignified self-portrait in profile with flowing hair and an inscription crowning him "Jacques Lipchitz sculptor" like a Roman emperor.

NOTES

1 H. Harvard Arnason, *Jacques Lipchitz: Sketches in Bronze* (New York: Praeger, 1969), 10.
2 Ibid.
3 Jacques Lipchitz and H. Harvard Arnason, *My Life in Sculpture* (New York: Viking Press, 1972), 29.
4 Ibid., 34.
5 Michael R. Taylor, "Jacques Lipchitz and Philadelphia," *Philadelphia Museum of Art Bulletin* 92, nos. 391–392 (2004): 21.
6 Lipchitz and Arnason 1972, 79.
7 Ibid., 103.
8 Taylor 2004, 35.
9 Lipchitz and Arnason 1972, 132.
10 Ibid.
11 Ibid., 140.
12 Ibid.
13 Arnason 1969, 20.
14 Lipchitz and Arnason 1972, 177.
15 Jacques Lipchitz, quoted in wall text of permanent display, curated by Tanya Sirakovich, The Israel Museum, Jerusalem, 2010.
16 Lipchitz told museum founder Ralph Goldman in the early 1960s that already in 1936 in Europe he had "wanted to do something for Palestine". Ralph Goldman in conversation with the author, 27 November 2011, Jerusalem.
17 When the final enlargement of *Our Tree of Life'* was made, Yulla Lipchitz went to the Lubbavitcher Rebbe for a blessing. While speaking with him, she expressed concern that the Phoenix was not a Jewish concept and thus questioned whether it belonged at the top of the work. The Rebbe sent his sexton to the basement storage room where his library was kept, and in five minutes he returned with a religious book which explained that the concept of a phoenix was a Jewish one and certainly appropriate for the work (Hanno Mott in an email to the author, 28 November 2011).
18 Arnason 1969, 26.
19 Lipchitz and Arnason 1972, 207.
20 Ibid., 225.
21 Dovid Zaklikowski, "How Jacques Lipchitz Found G-d: The Rabbi and the Sculptor," http://www.chabad.org/therebbe/article_cdo/aid/393257/jewish/How-Jacques-Lipchitz Found-G-d.htm (accessed: 21 March 2024).

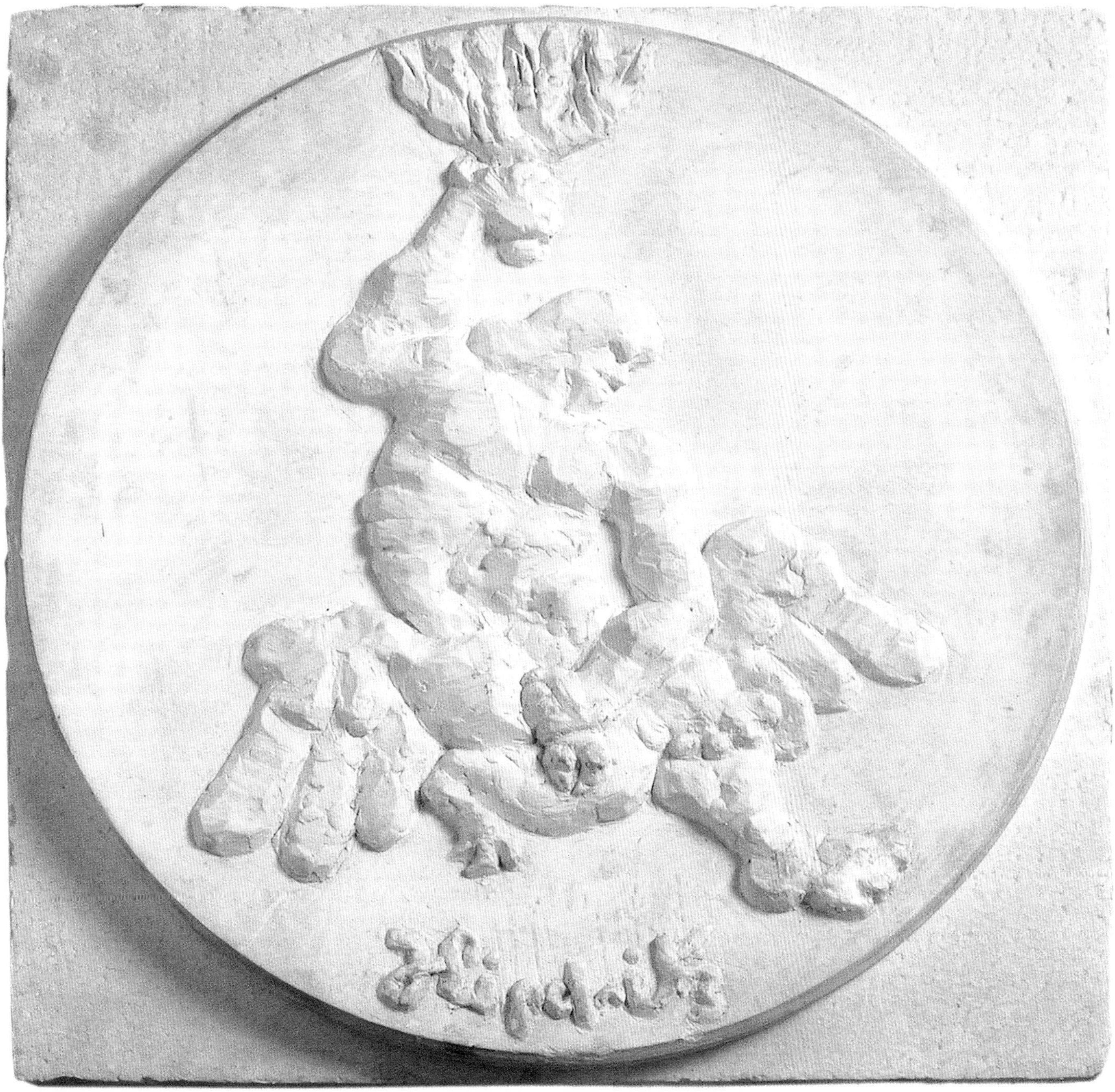
J. Lipchitz

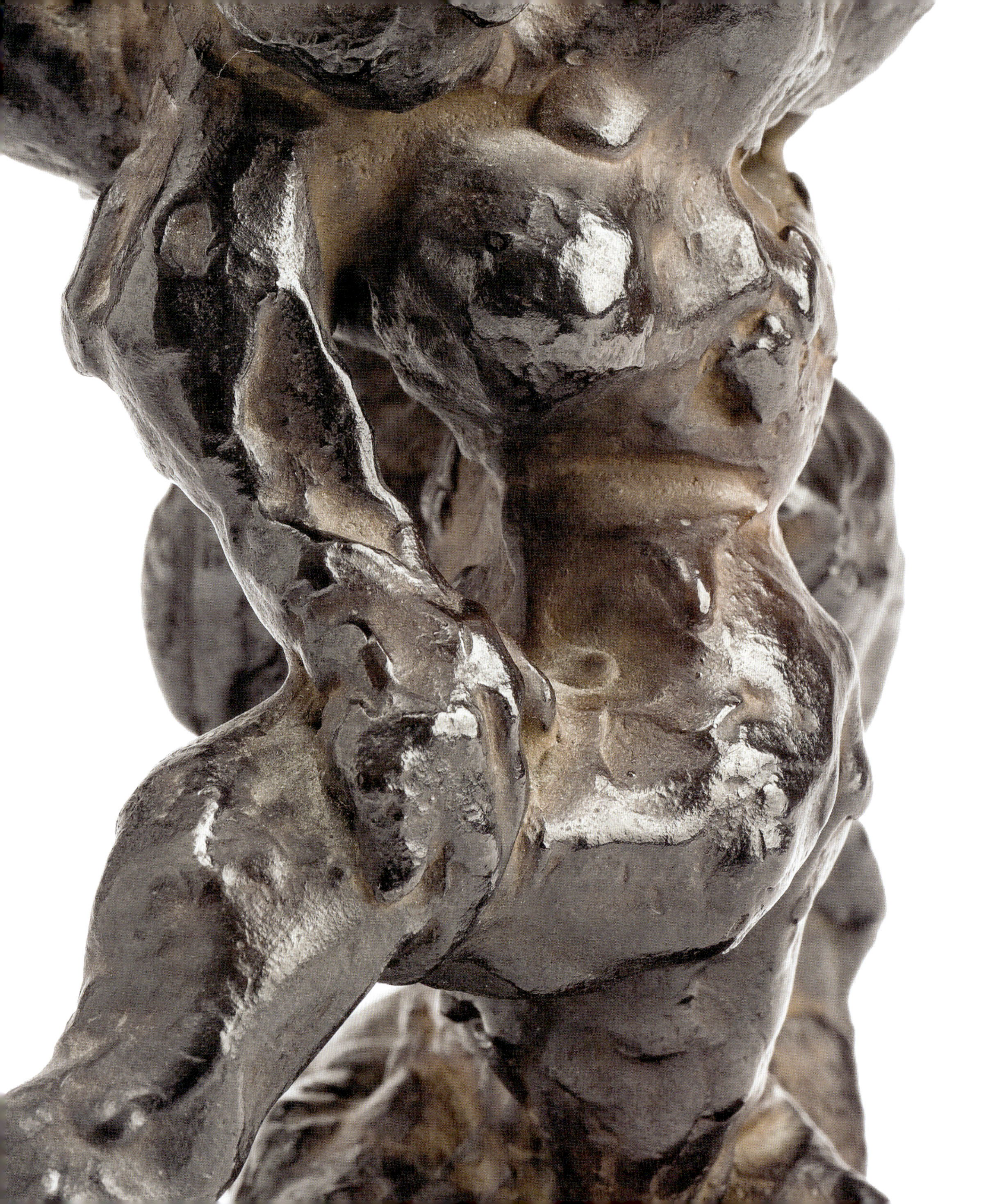

CATALOGUE

ABBREVIATIONS

Signed l. l.: lower left
l. r.: lower right
u. l.: upper left
u. r.: upper right
Wilkinson cat.: Wilkinson, Alan G. *The Sculpture of Jacques Lipchitz. A Catalogue Raisonné. The Paris Years, 1910–1940*, vol. 1 (London: Thames & Hudson, 1996); *The American Years, 1941–1973*, vol. 2 (New York: Thames & Hudson, 2000).

KB: Kata Bodor
MO: Márton Orosz
AS: Anett Somodi
DS: Dominika Sodics

Detail of cat. 16

Cat. 1

JACQUES LIPCHITZ
(Druskininkai, 1891 – Capri, 1973)
Seated Pierrot, 1922
Lead, 34 × 14.2 × 13.5 cm
Signed: J.L. 3/7., 22.
Private collection
Wilkinson cat. 136

Through his experiments with forms and materials in 1915–1916, Lipchitz arrived at complete abstraction, but he felt that he had meanwhile lost sight of the human element and man's connection to nature, which had always been important to him.[1] He therefore, whilst remaining within the cubist framework, gradually returned to the principles he considered so essential. Among the figures he depicted, those of Harlequin and Pierrot playing musical instruments appeared increasingly often from 1919 onwards, in numerous variations. Characters from the commedia dell'arte feature in the works of other cubist artists, notably Pablo Picasso and Juan Gris. This can be attributed in part to the rediscovery of and newfound fashion for eighteenth-century French painting, in particular the art of Jean-Antoine Watteau. In 1922 Lipchitz modelled a sequence of seated figures, one being the *Seated Pierrot*, consisting of weighty masses in simplified rectangular shapes, although the lines are softer than in his earlier cubist sculptures, the edges more rounded. While in later years he progressively shifted away from cubism towards a more diffuse, baroque-like mode of expression, he described himself as a cubist his entire life.

[AS]

1 Jacques Lipchitz and H. Harvard Arnason, *My Life in Sculpture* (New York: The Viking Press, 1972), 33.

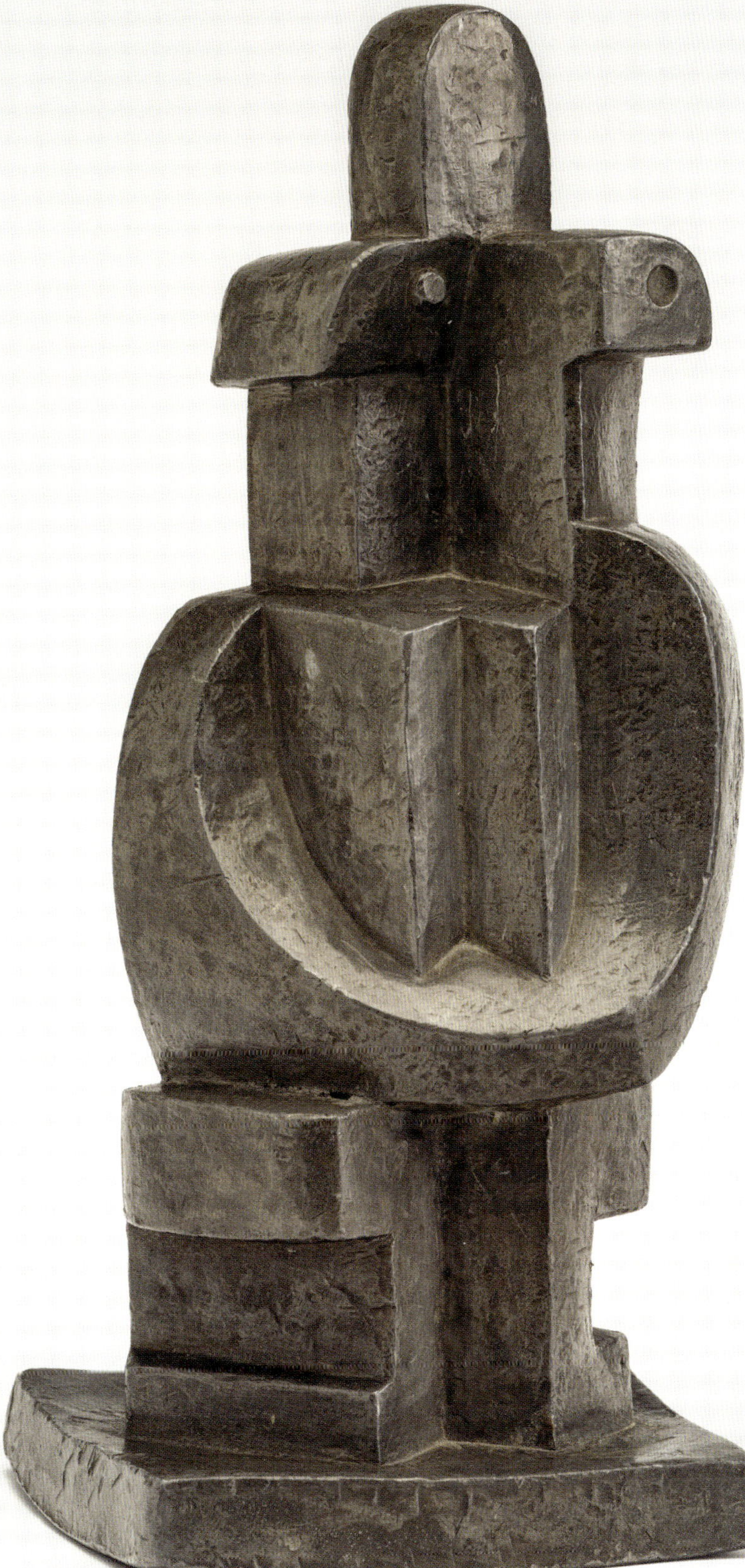

Cat. 2

JACQUES LIPCHITZ
(Druskininkai, 1891 – Capri, 1973)
Woman with a Guitar, 1923–1924
Bronze, 15.7 × 23.1 × 3.8 cm
Signed: J.L. 6/7; foundry stamp: Georges Rudier. Fondeur. Paris.
Private collection
Wilkinson cat. 150

In 1922, through Paul Guillaume, Lipchitz met the wealthy American businessman and art collector Dr Albert C. Barnes.[1] Barnes purchased eight sculptures from Lipchitz and commissioned him to make a series of bas-reliefs for the facade of his new foundation building in Philadelphia. A relief of 1918 entitled *Still Life with Musical Instruments* had caught the collector's eye, so Lipchitz's reliefs for the facade, designed in 1922–1923, explore the theme of music and the connection between the figure and the instrument. This subject had first appeared in his sculpture as early as 1914 (*Sailor with Guitar*, Philadelphia Museum of Art, Philadelphia), but in the 1920s he frequently turned to the theme, as did, in their cubist periods, Pablo Picasso, Henri Laurens, and Juan Gris. There are numerous variants of the bronze relief *Woman with a Guitar*, but it is perhaps here that he most succeeded in unifying the figure and her instrument into what is essentially a "figure-guitar". The bronze was cast in the Rudier foundry in Paris, and the original plaster version of 1923 is now in the collection of the Krannert Art Museum (Champaign, Illinois), courtesy of the Jacques and Yulla Lipchitz Foundation.

[AS]

1 Jacques Lipchitz and H. Harvard Arnason, *My Life in Sculpture* (New York: The Viking Press, 1972), 70.

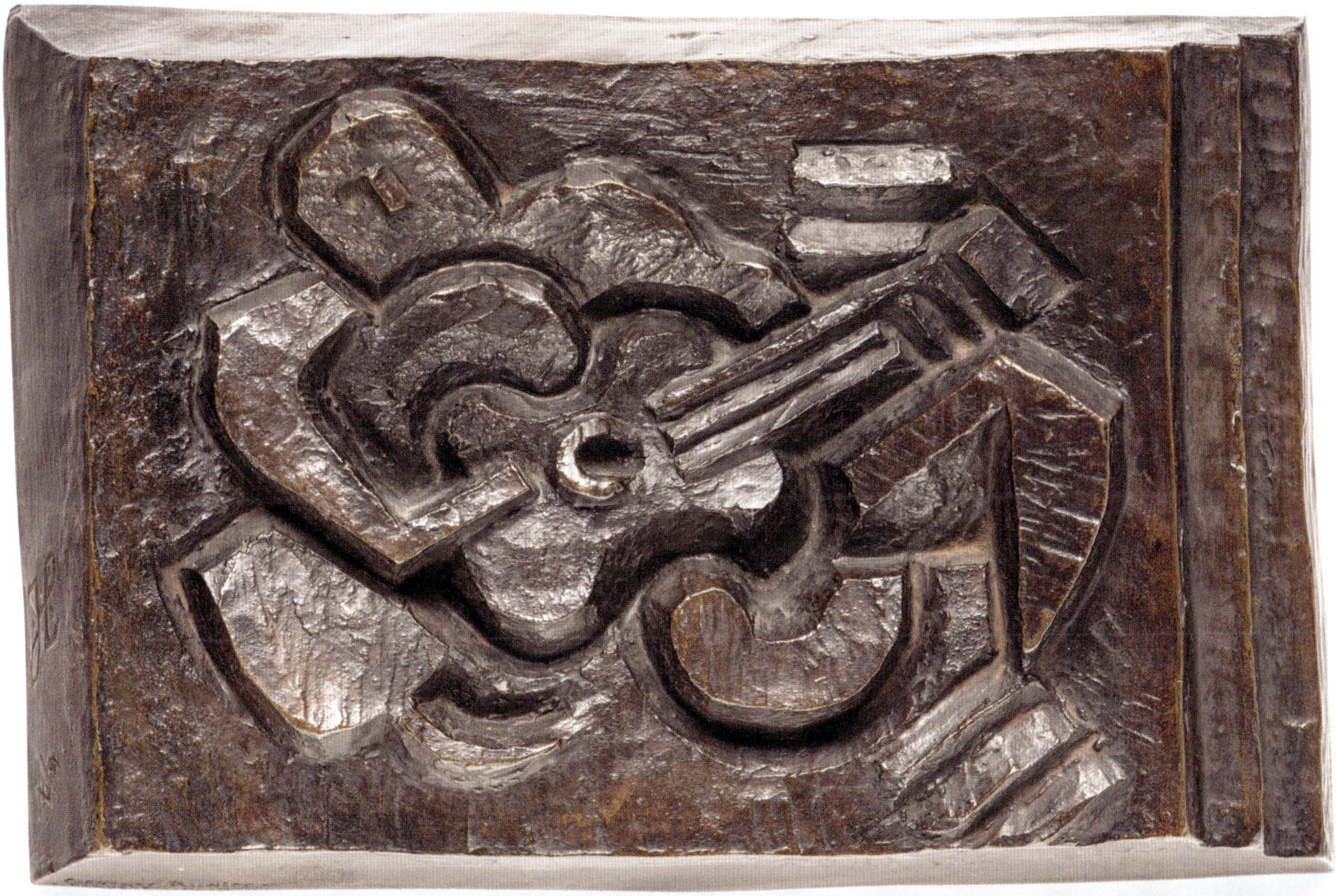

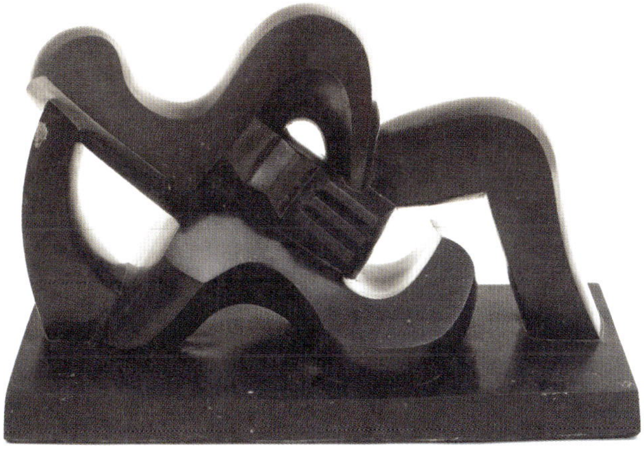

16 Jacques Lipchitz
Reclining Nude with Guitar, 1928
The Museum of Modern Art,
New York, Blanchette Hooker
Rockefeller Bequest

Cat. 3

JACQUES LIPCHITZ
(Druskininkai, 1891 – Capri, 1973)
Sculpture Design (Figure with a Guitar), early 1920s (?)
Pen and ink on paper, 193 × 80 mm
Private collection

Throughout his more than sixty-year career, Lipchitz worked with a limited set of motifs, although he generated a wealth of variations on certain themes. In recording his initial idea and its subsequent continuous reworkings, he relied heavily on drawing. The variations not only vividly reveal his experimentation with form, but also convey his desire to execute his works at a monumental scale. While he was denied the opportunity to do so during his cubist period, the sketch shown here suggests that he was already considering the possibility. Around 1920 he made numerous versions of a figure playing the guitar, one of the favourite motifs in the iconography of cubism. In this period the artist was intensely concerned with the challenges inherent in creating a cubist sculpture in the round and integrating it into the surrounding space, and so as well as reliefs — including the work entitled *Woman with a Guitar* (cat. 2) — he also produced a number of free-standing versions. The further development of his thinking is documented in this drawing, which shows the figure with the guitar now placed upon a pedestal. The rounded lines in the composition indicate that by the early 1920s Lipchitz was toning down his strict geometric style.

[DS]

побегаю ш...

стенка буд...

и прислать

в крайне ...

затруднить,

но без этой

нельзя оба...

без этой б...

не могу нача...

процедура

иногда по...

Пока все ...

за при...

Поклон ...

Даша все по ...

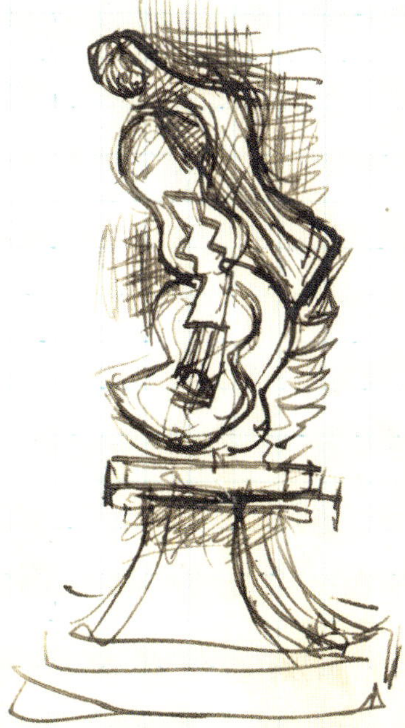

1908 год

Cat. 4

ANDRÉ LHOTE
(Bordeaux, 1885 – Paris, 1962)
Night Party in Montparnasse, at the Bal Bullier, 1922
Colour lithograph on paper, 1380 × 990 mm
Private collection

Known as a leading exponent of cubist painting, André Lhote began his career as a sculptor. Painting predominated in his art after his move to Paris in 1906. He also excelled as a theorist and a teacher. In 1929 he delivered a lecture at the National Salon in Budapest, where four of his works were exhibited. In 1922, the year he produced this poster, he opened his own art academy in Montparnasse. Located nearby was the Bal Bullier, a nightclub designed in an oriental style, famed as one of the main haunts of Paris's Bohemian art world. Lhote's poster was made for a costume ball held at the club. Its decorative composition, created from an artfully arranged fabric of visual elements, relies on simple yet eye-catching devices. The colour scheme is limited to the black and gold making up the lettering and the chequered clothing of the figure. For this groundbreaking typographical game, the artist utilised the harlequin figure from his earlier painting entitled *Homage to Watteau*. The tableau, comprising enlarged initials placed in alphabetical order, lists the names of the avantgarde artists helping to organise the ball, including that of Lhote's friend, Jacques Lipchitz.

[MO]

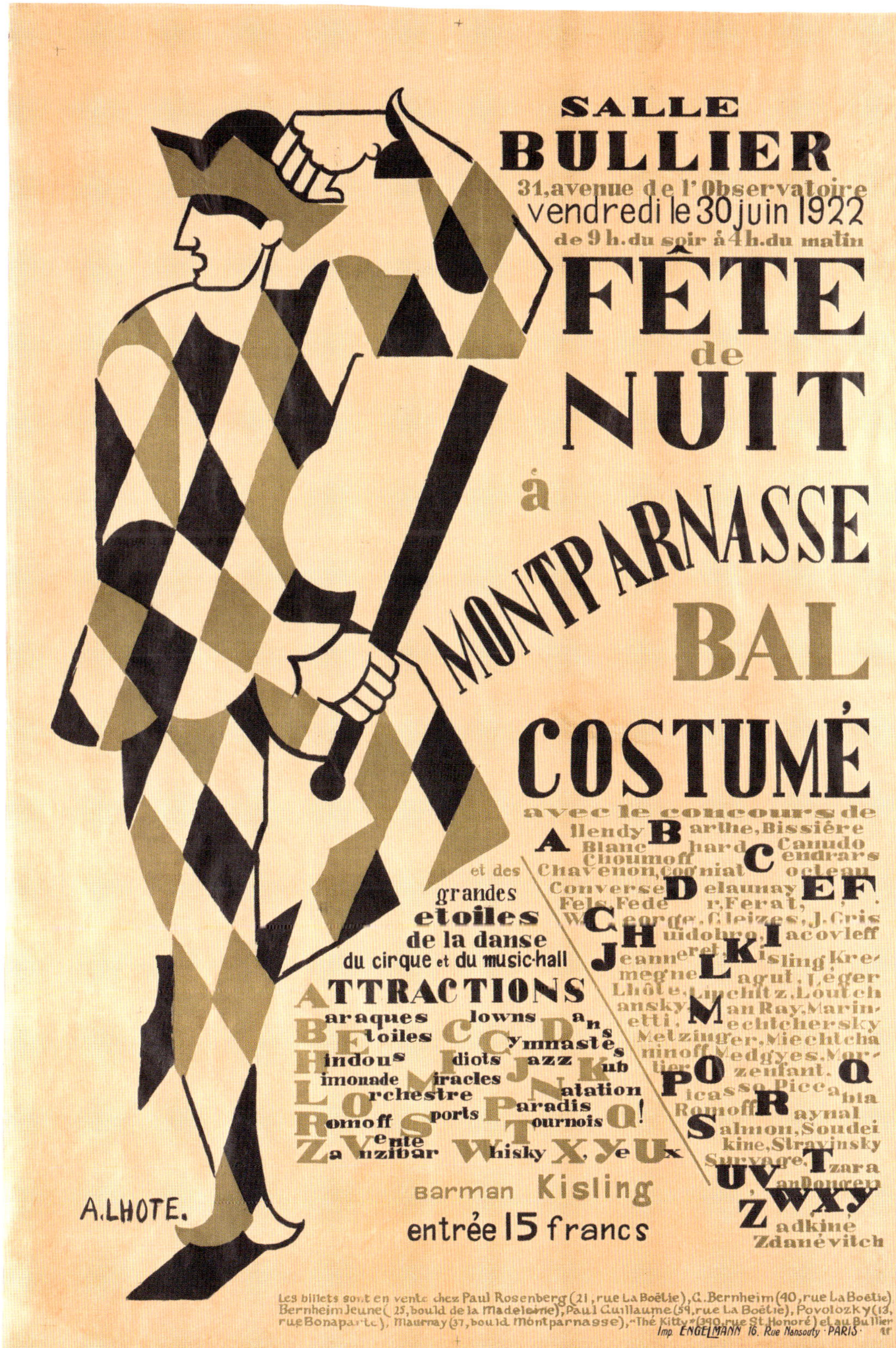
SALLE
BULLIER
31, avenue de l'Observatoire
vendredi le 30 juin 1922
de 9 h. du soir à 4 h. du matin
FÊTE
de
NUIT
à
MONTPARNASSE
BAL
COSTUMÉ
avec le concours de
et des
grandes
etoiles
de la danse
du cirque et du music-hall
ATTRACTIONS
barman Kisling
entrée 15 francs
A. LHOTE.
Les billets sont en vente chez Paul Rosenberg (21, rue La Boëtie), G. Bernheim (40, rue La Boëtie) Bernheim Jeune (25, bould de la Madeleine), Paul Guillaume (59, rue La Boëtie), Povolozky (13, rue Bonaparte), Maurnay (37, bould Montparnasse), «Thé Kitty» (390, rue St Honoré) et au Bullier
Imp. ENGELMANN 16. Rue Nansouty · PARIS ·

Cat. 5

JACQUES LIPCHITZ
(Druskininkai, 1891 – Capri, 1973)
Towards a New World, maquette no. 4, 1934
Bronze, 19.3 × 19.2 × 8 cm
Signed: Lipchitz 5/7
Private collection
Wilkinson cat. 321

In 1934 Lipchitz produced maquettes for a sculpture entitled *Towards a New World*, which was ultimately never executed. The composition, reworking the iconic motif of the flag-bearer, reflects what the artist later described as his "momentary enthusiasm for the revolutionary cause in Russia".[1] The sketch can be linked to another work of 1934 conceived in a similar spirit, his planned monument celebrating "the liberation of the Russian people through industry and agriculture",[2] although the sketches he sent to the Soviet Union were rejected.

From the early 1930s onwards, Lipchitz observed European political radicalisation with growing concern, and this was reflected ever more emphatically in his works. In search for alternatives to the troubling far-right ideologies, the artist initially sympathised with the ideals of the socialist revolution, although after visiting his siblings in the Soviet Union in 1935, his utopian dreams were shattered. Recollecting what he had seen in Moscow, he declared, "I have always been and continued to be on the side of freedom and against any form of oppression or dictatorship".[3]

[DS]

1 Jacques Lipchitz and H. Harvard Arnason, *My Life in Sculpture* (New York: The Viking Press, 1972), 132.
2 Ibid., 131.
3 Ibid., 132.

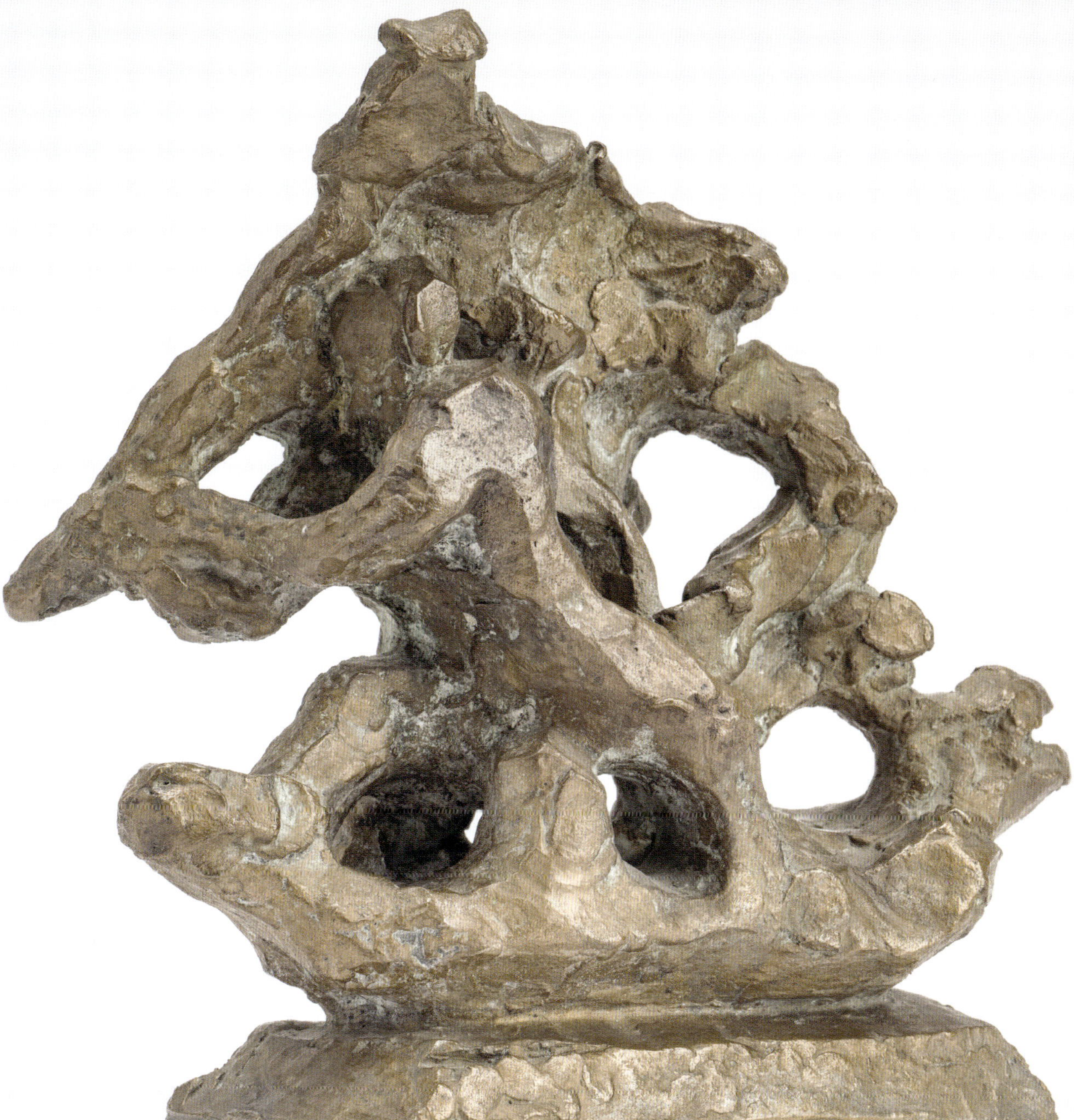

Cat. 6

JACQUES LIPCHITZ
(Druskininkai, 1891 – Capri, 1973)
Prometheus and the Vulture
Pages from the portfolio: Jacques Lipchitz, *12 dessins pour Prométhée* (Paris: Jeanne Bucher, 1940)
Collotype prints with pochoir on paper, approximately 420 × 310 mm
Private collection

In 1936, the French government commissioned a monumental sculpture from Lipchitz for the following year's Exposition Internationale in Paris. The artist had long been fascinated with the mythological figure of Prometheus, known for stealing fire from Olympus and giving it to humanity. As punishment, Zeus had Prometheus chained to a rock, to have his liver devoured by an eagle every day for eternity. Lipchitz developed his ideas in a series of preparatory drawings, ultimately discarding Prometheus victorious, brandishing a torch, in favour of the titan grappling with his torturer: in the artist's reworking, a vulture rather than an eagle.

The figure of Prometheus was conceptually ideal for the sculpture's intended setting, the Science Pavilion, but to Lipchitz it also conveyed universal meaning, embodying the "struggle between day and night, good and bad, progress and retrogression".[1] In the face of the political situation in Europe at the time, the depiction of Prometheus's struggle was reinterpreted as a defiant stand against Nazism: to underline the message, Prometheus is wearing a Phrygian cap, symbol of liberty and democracy. In the midst of attacks from the right-wing press, in 1940 the artist's friend and gallerist Jeanne Bucher published a portfolio of drawings made for the Prometheus sculpture; the works presented here come from this album.

[DS]

1 Cited in: Bert van Bork, *Jacques Lipchitz. The Artist at Work* (New York: Crown Publishers, 1966), 14.

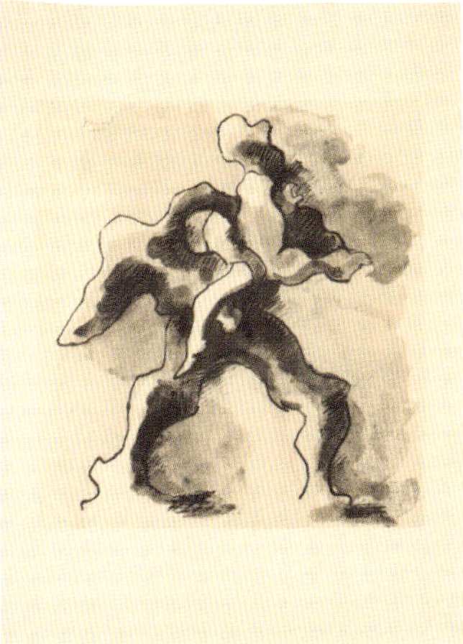
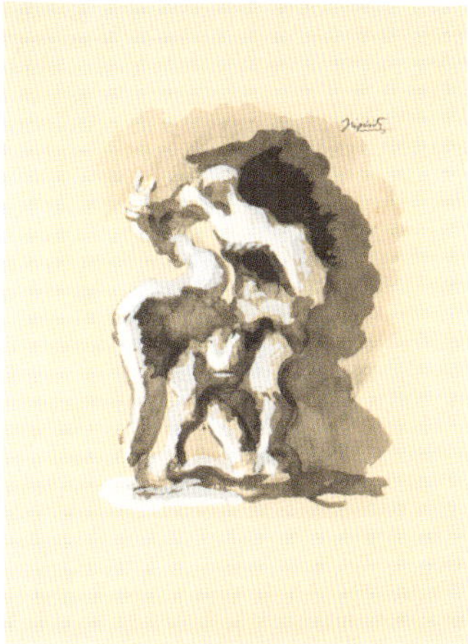
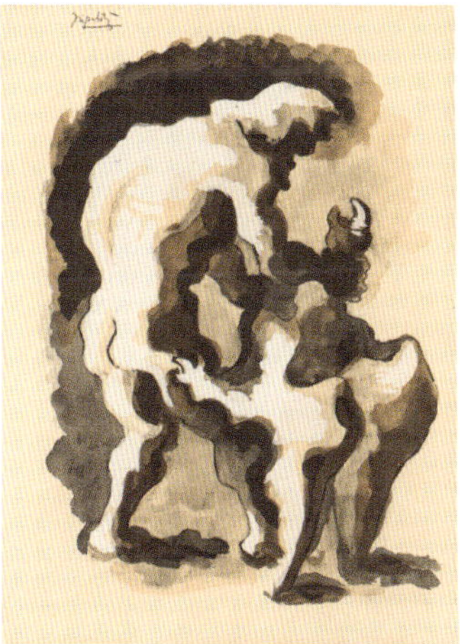
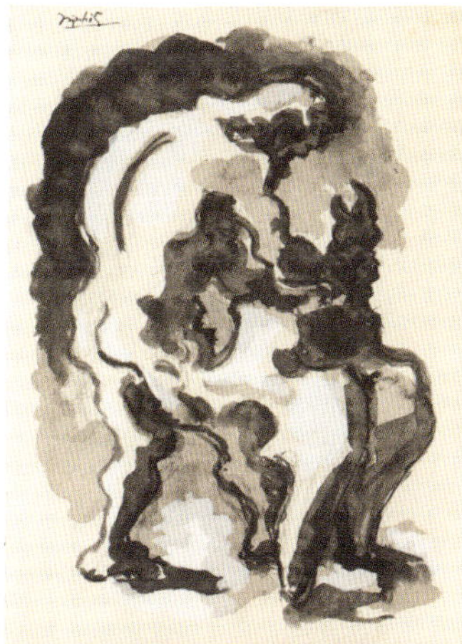
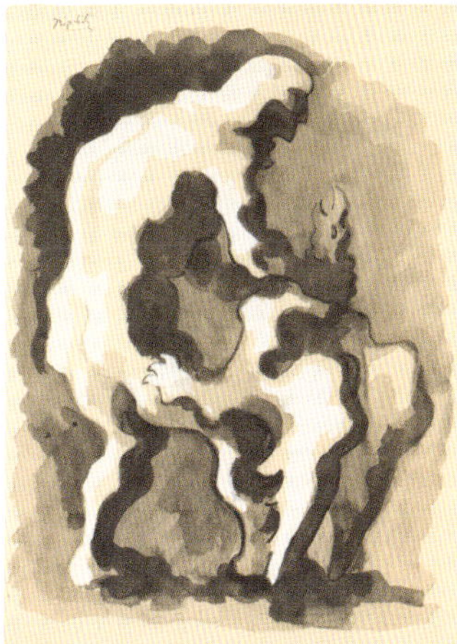
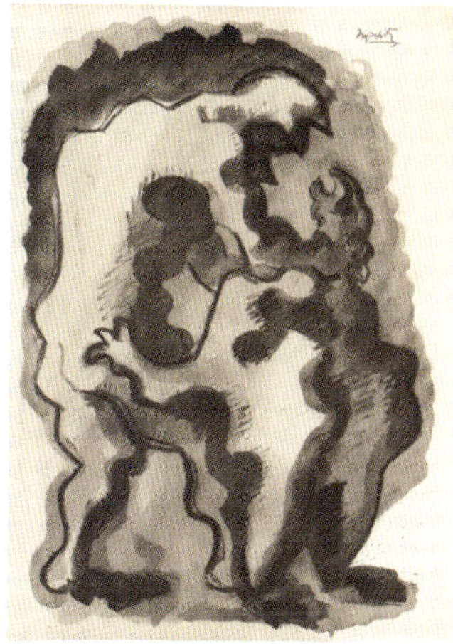
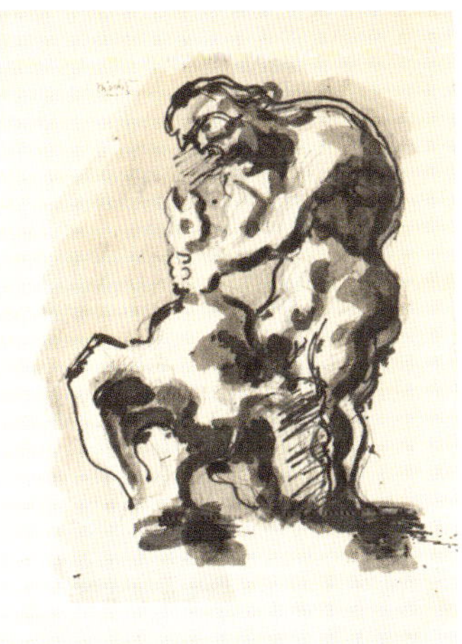
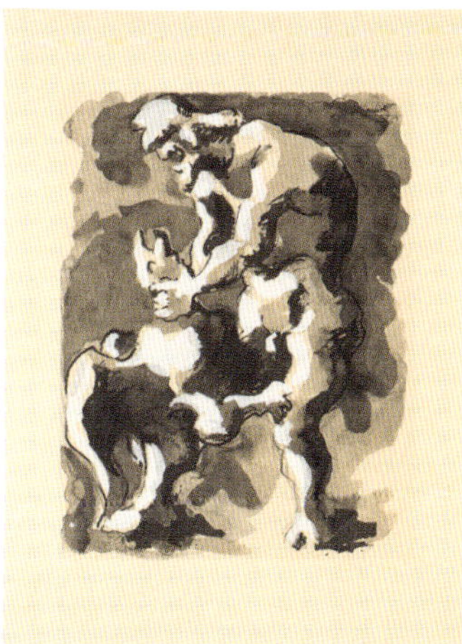
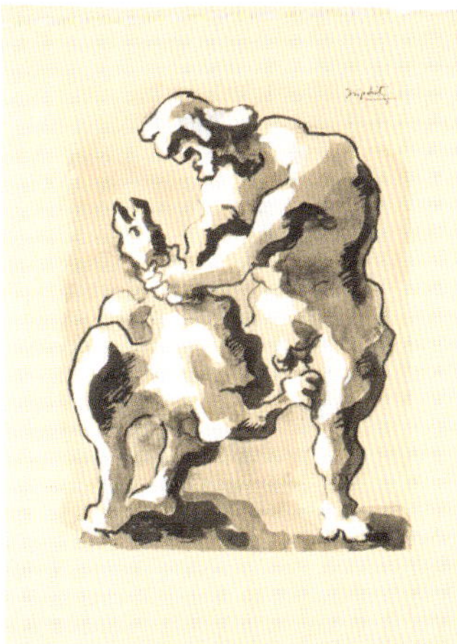
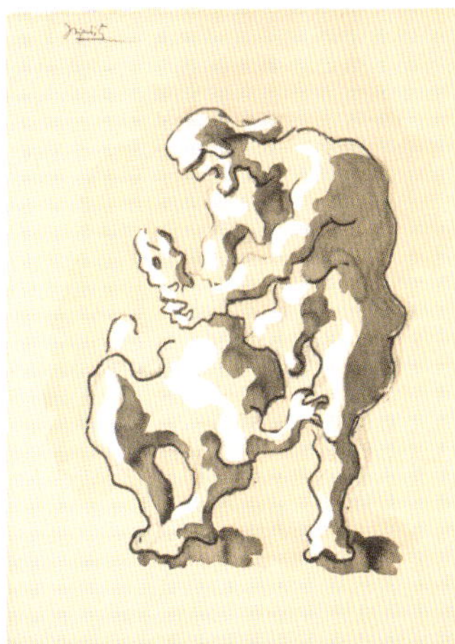

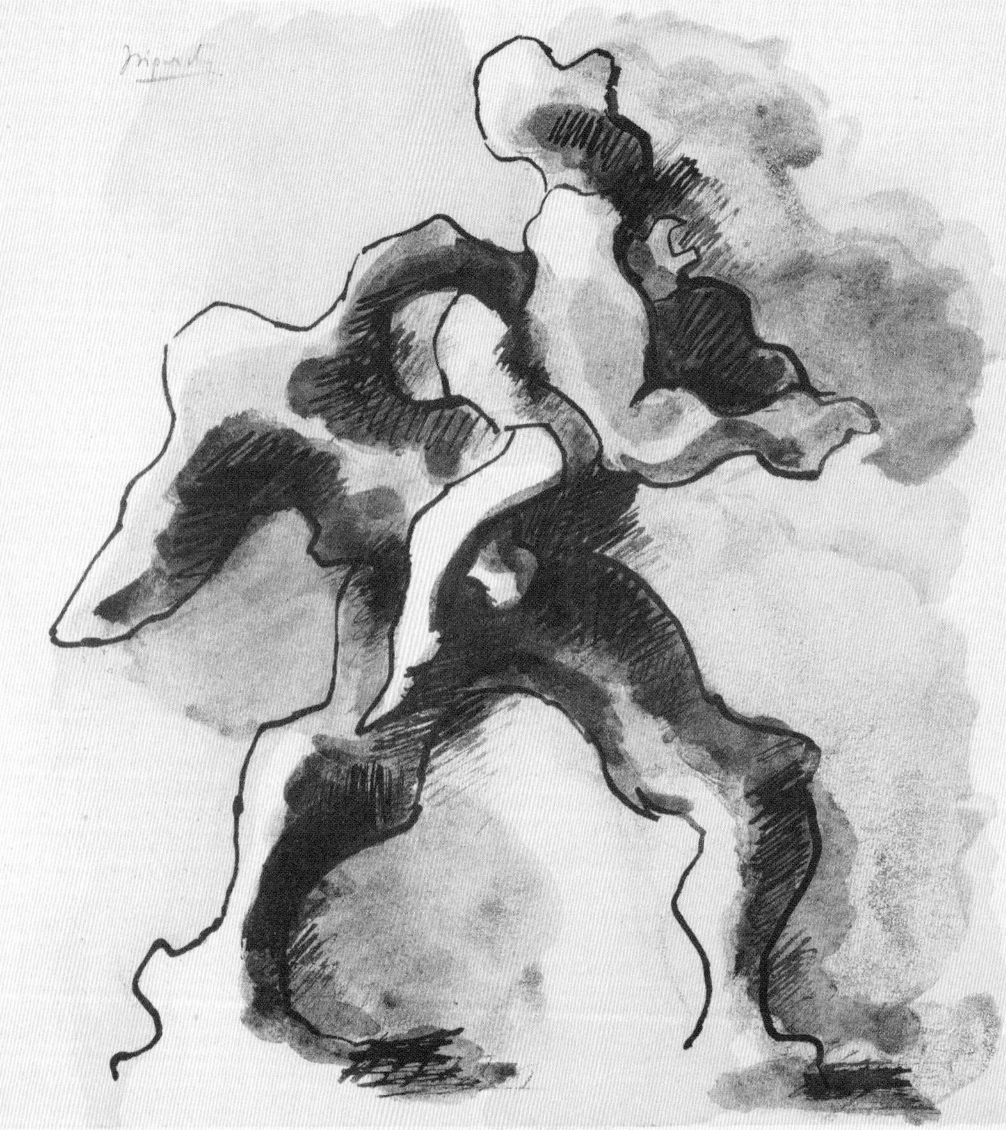

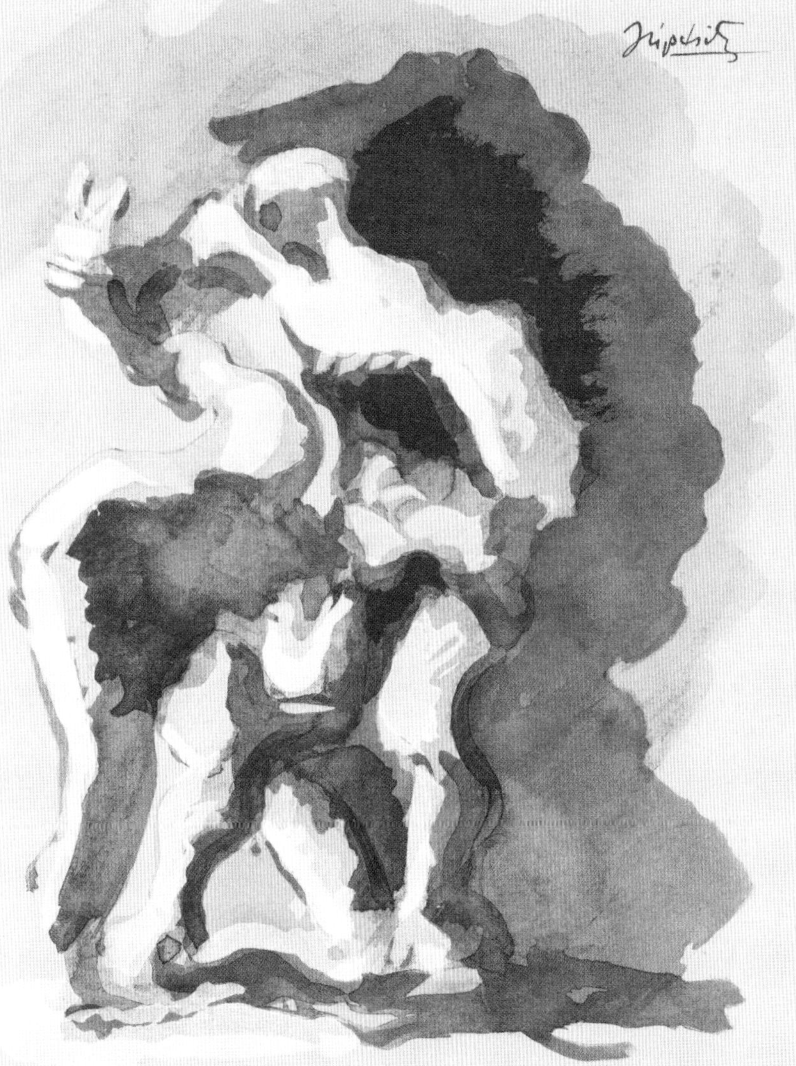

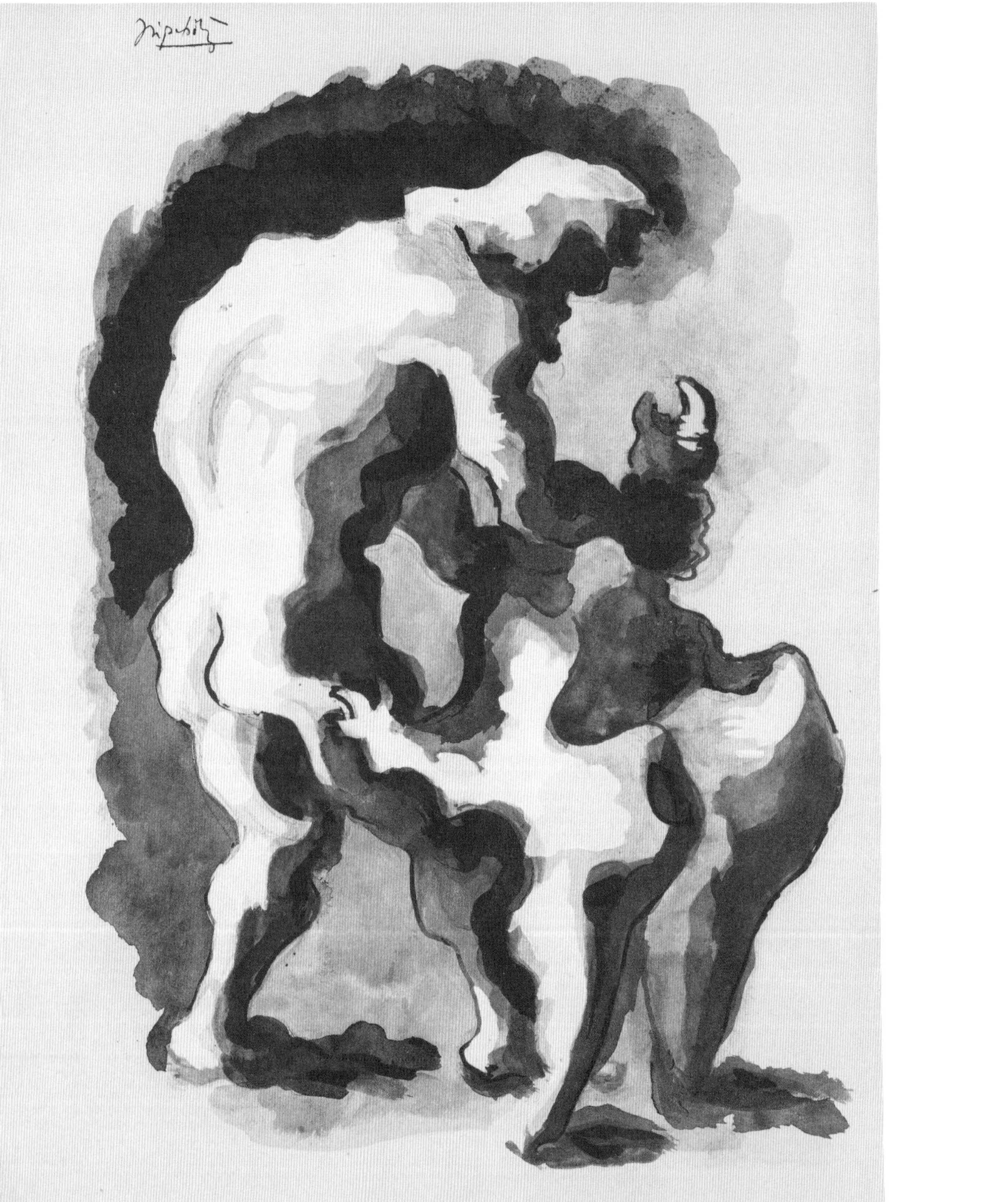

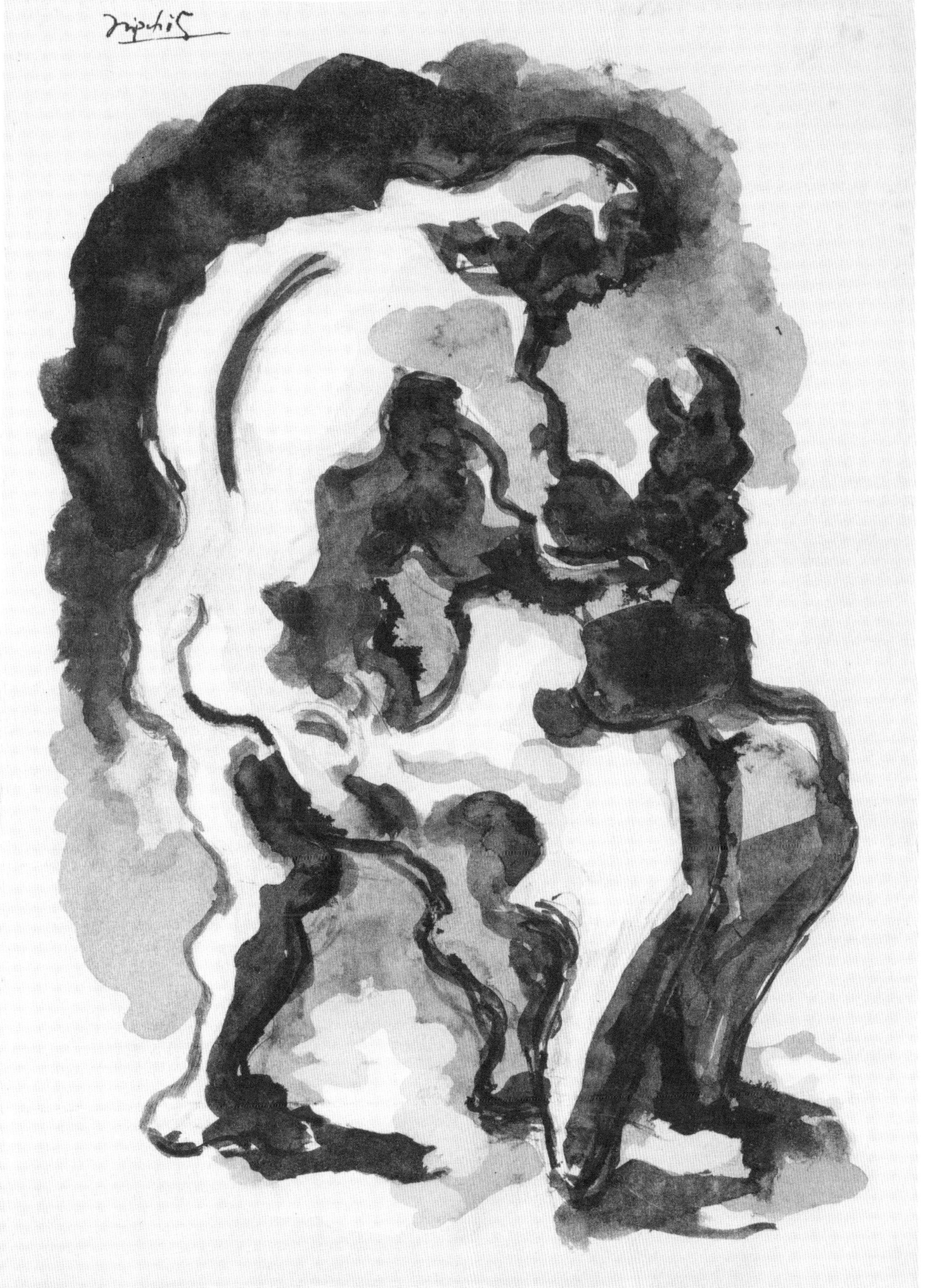

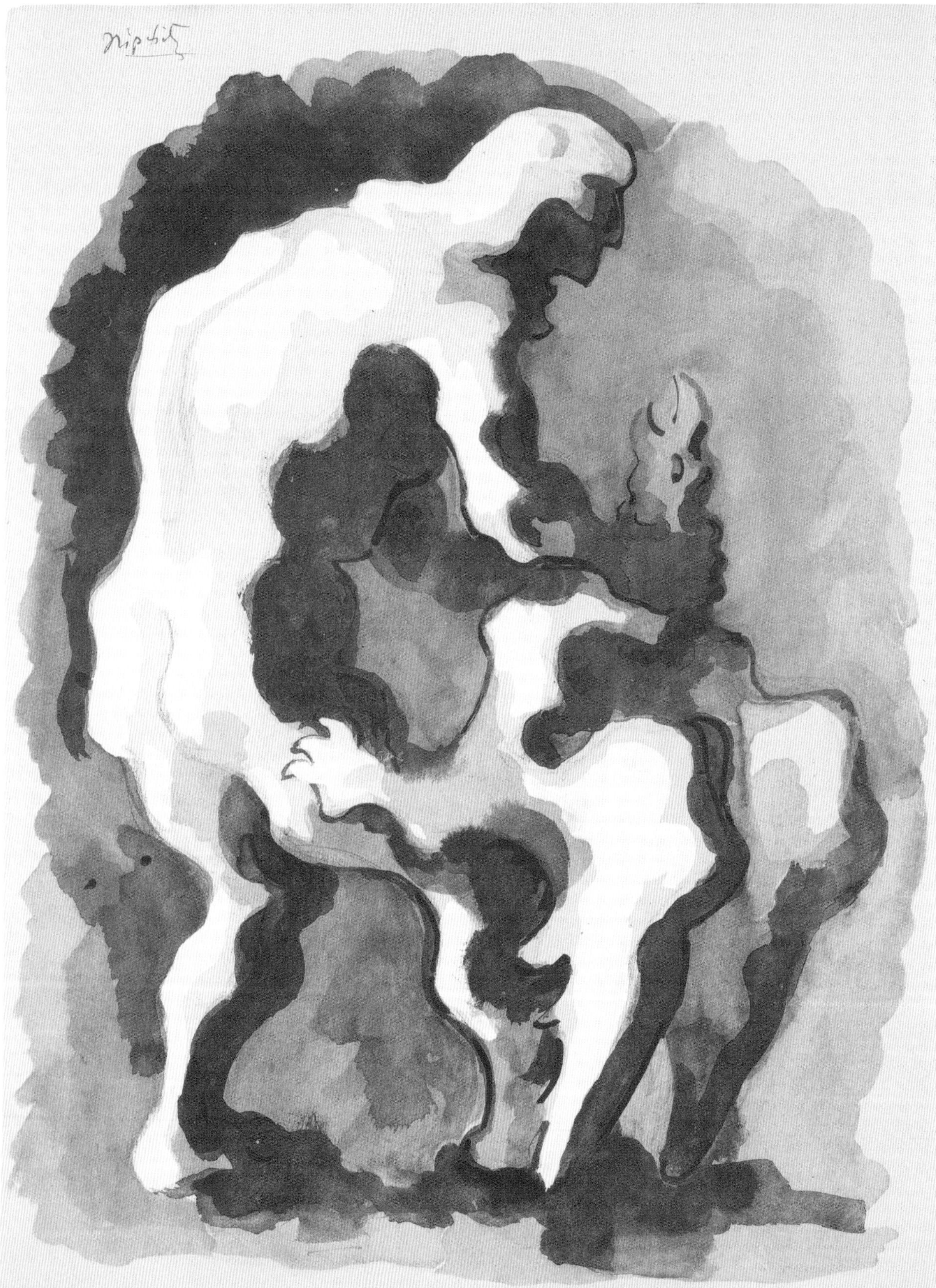

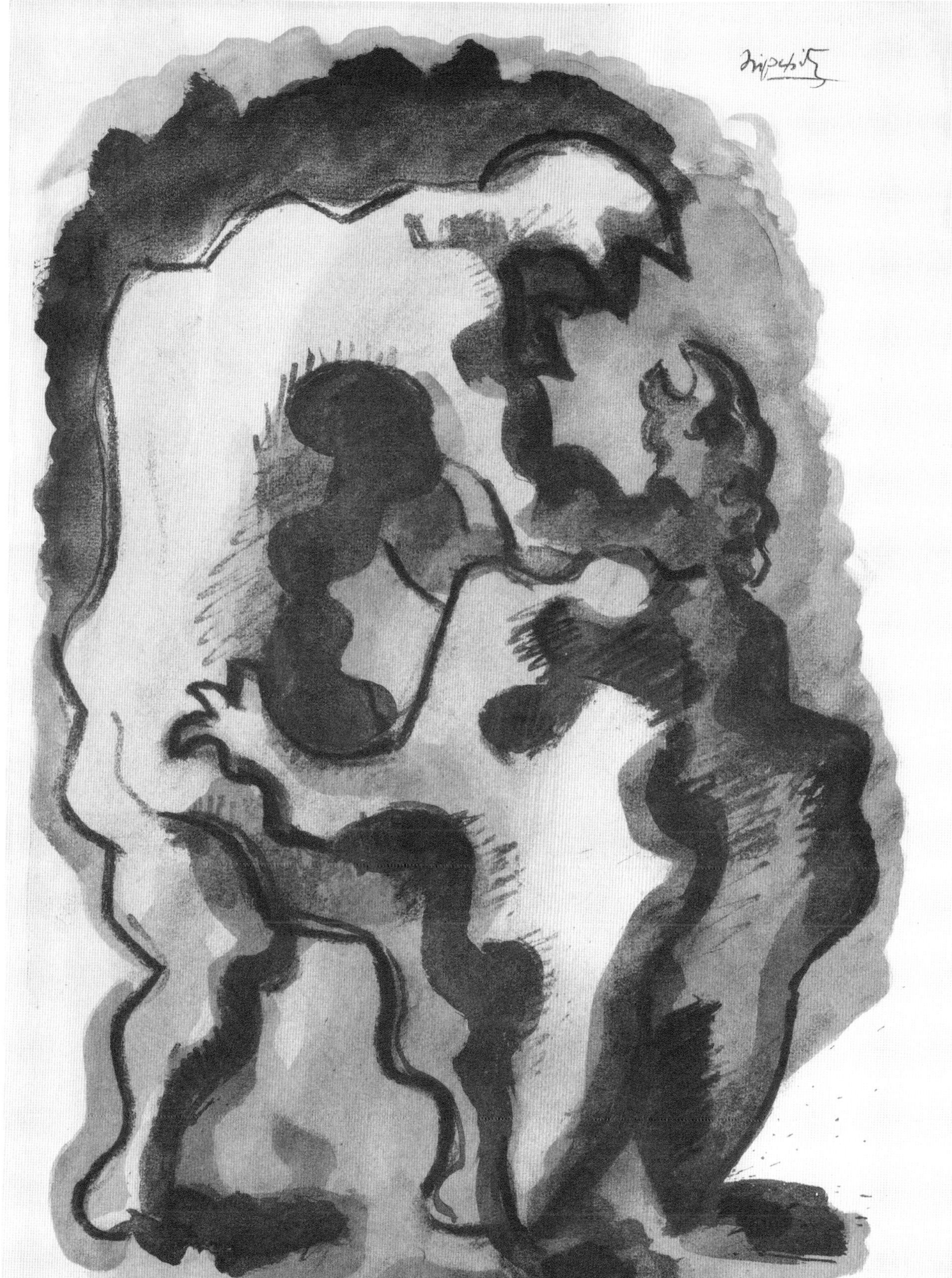

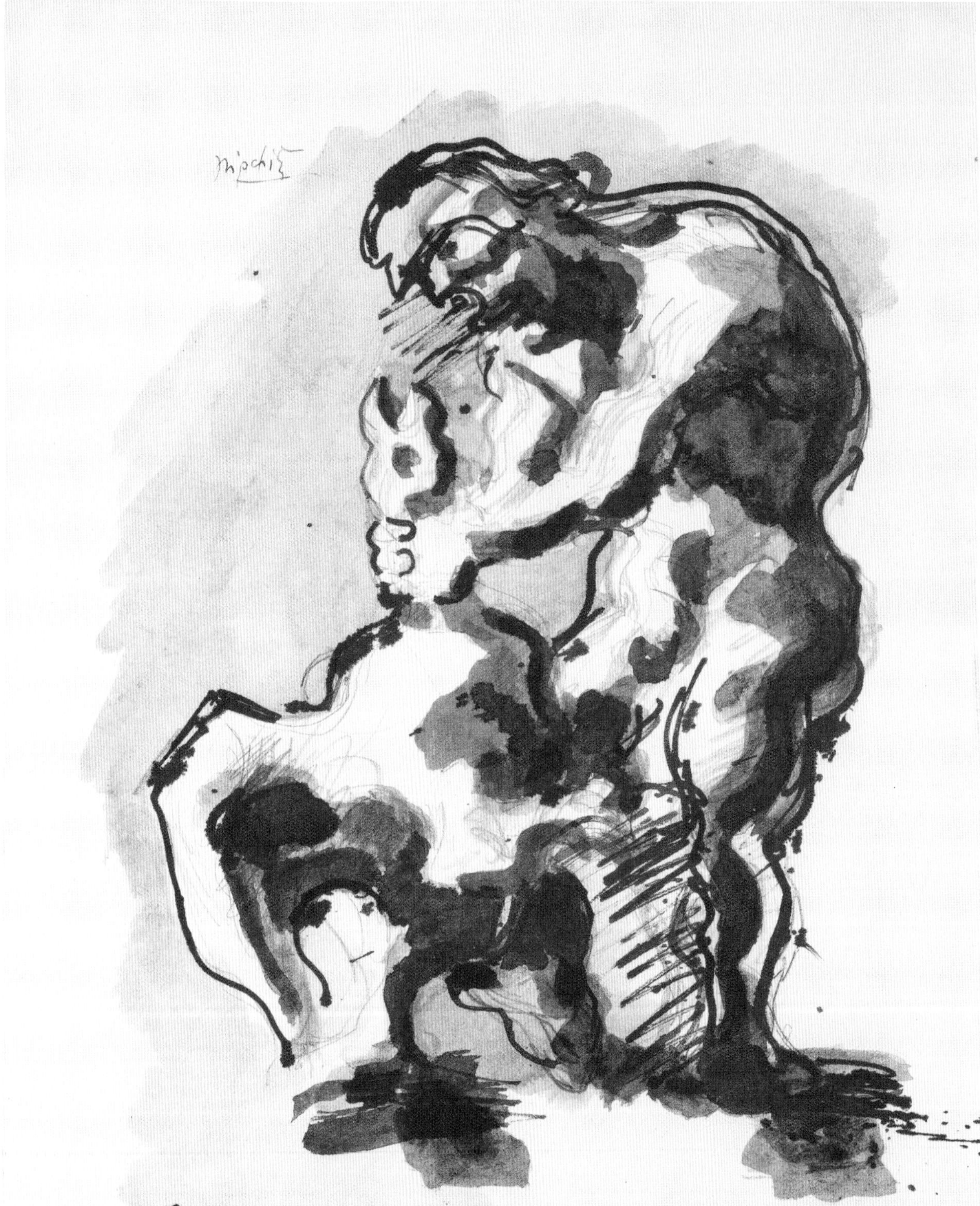

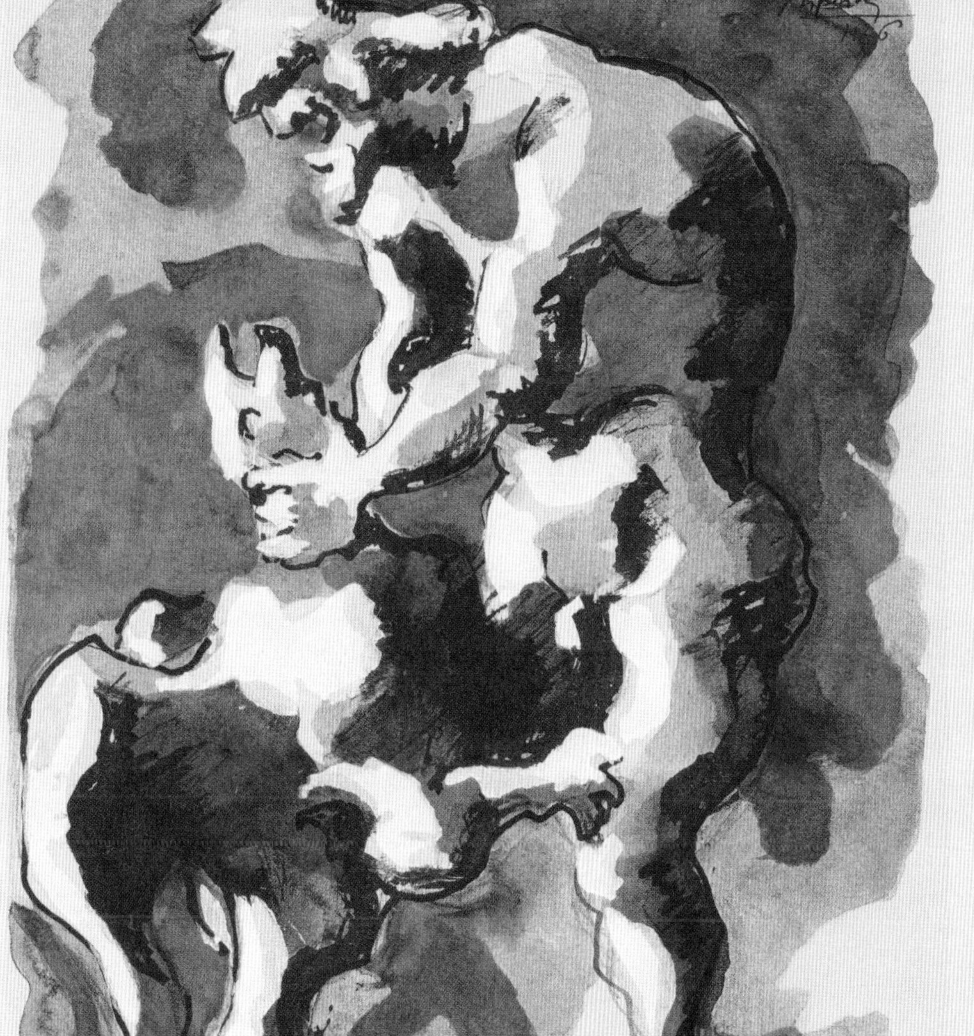

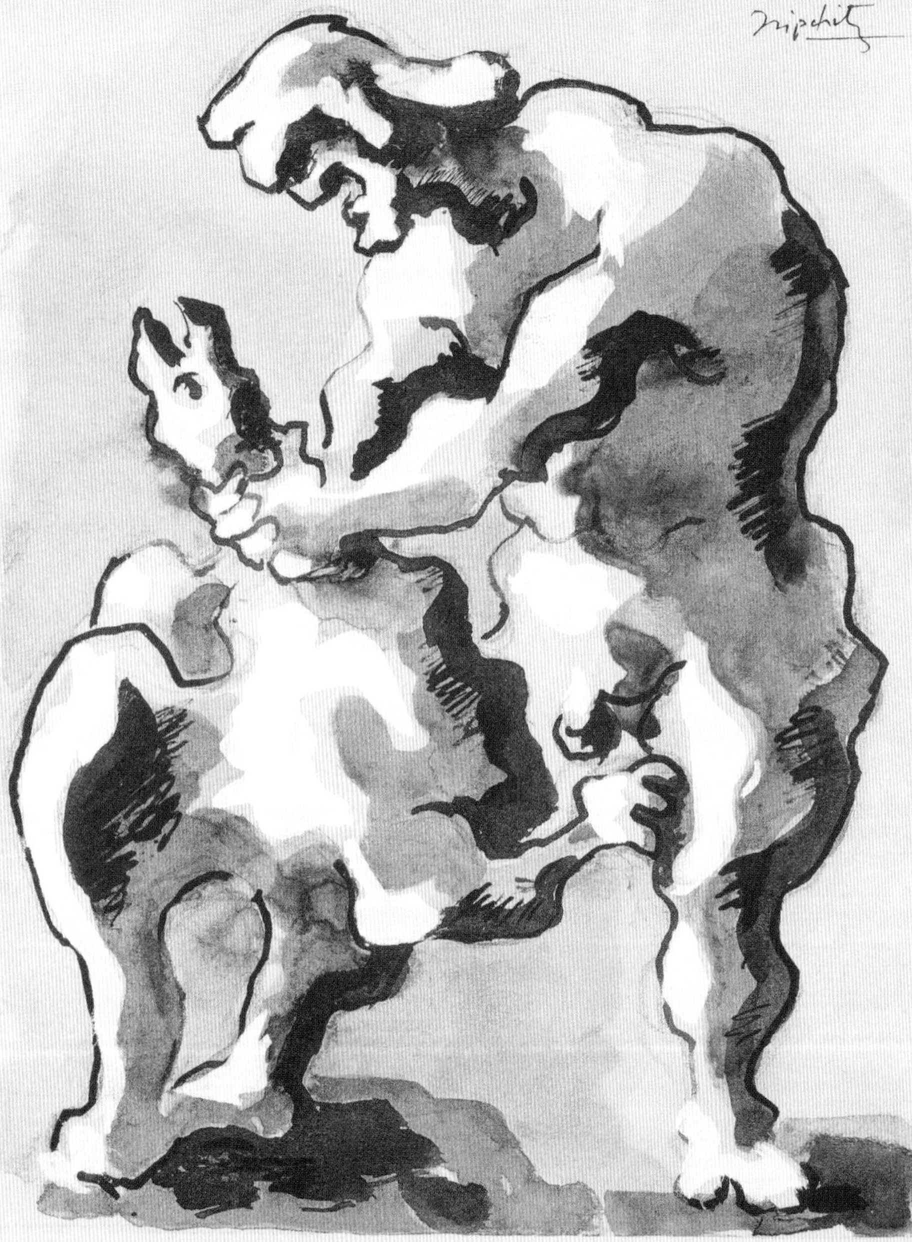

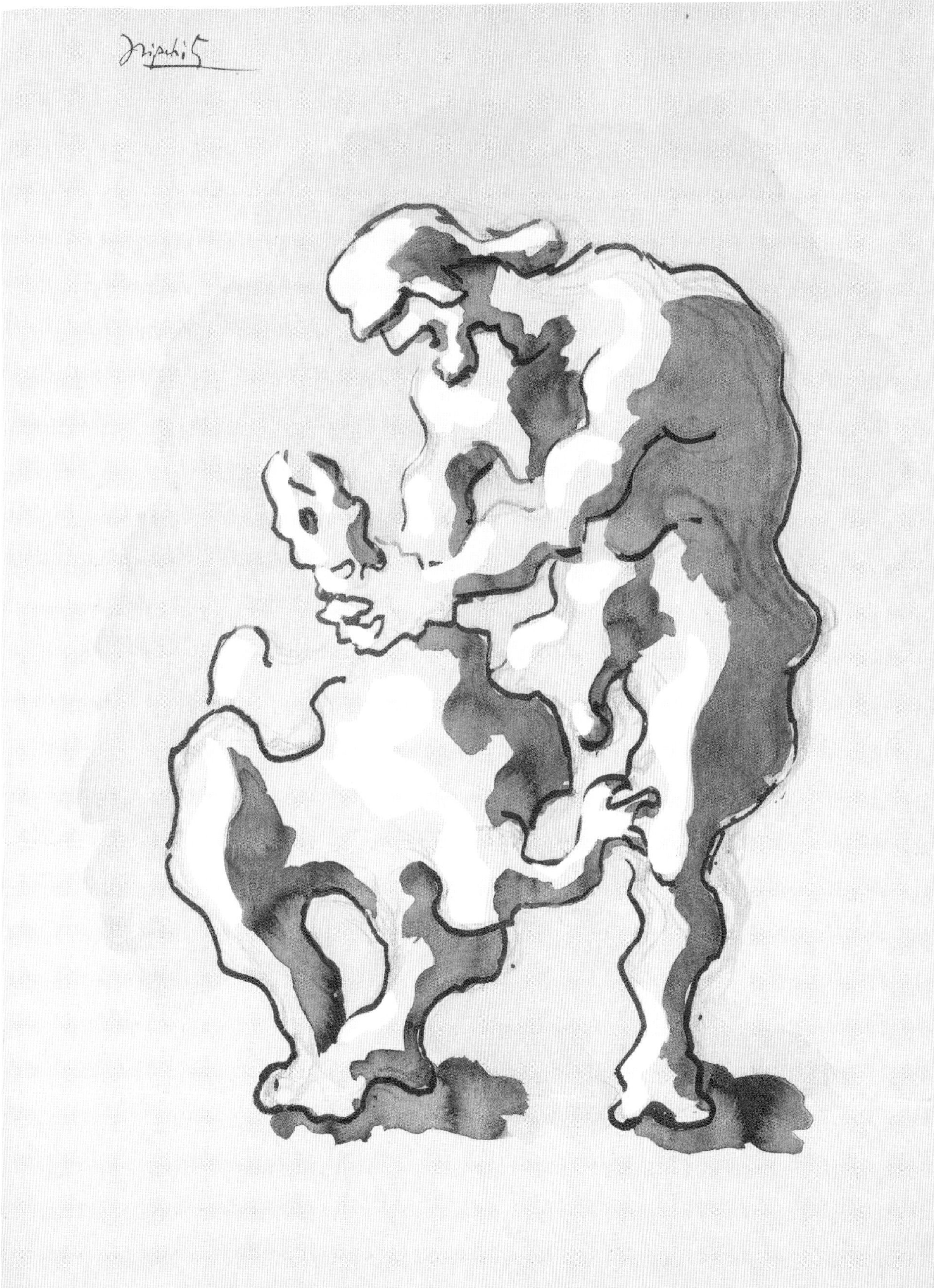

Cat. 7

JACQUES LIPCHITZ
(Druskininkai, 1891 – Capri, 1973)
Theseus and the Minotaur, 1943
Aquatint on paper, 566 × 380 mm
Signed l. r.: Lipchitz; l. l.: 28/50
Private collection

An oft-recurring motif in Lipchitz's œuvre is the bull. The artist was inspired by a Peruvian folk custom he had heard about, in which thrill-seeking crowds watched the brutal combat between a bull and a condor. Besides the South American tradition, Lipchitz also found inspiration in classical mythology: the bull appears in his sculptures and paper-based works dealing with the Rape of Europa and with the story of Theseus defeating the Cretan monster, the Minotaur. During World War II, both myths took on political meaning. Like Zeus in the form of a bull, the human-bodied, bull-headed Minotaur represents Hitler, while his vanquisher, Theseus, was specifically identified by the artist with Charles de Gaulle, a key figure in the French Resistance. In Lipchitz's compositions, Theseus and the Minotaur are almost fused together, the hero simultaneously fighting the outside world and the internal enemy. As the artist said, it is "as though there were a Hitler in each of us whom we must destroy. Theseus is killing a part of himself".[1]

[DS]

1 Jacques Lipchitz and H. Harvard Arnason, *My Life in Sculpture* (New York: The Viking Press, 1972), 159.

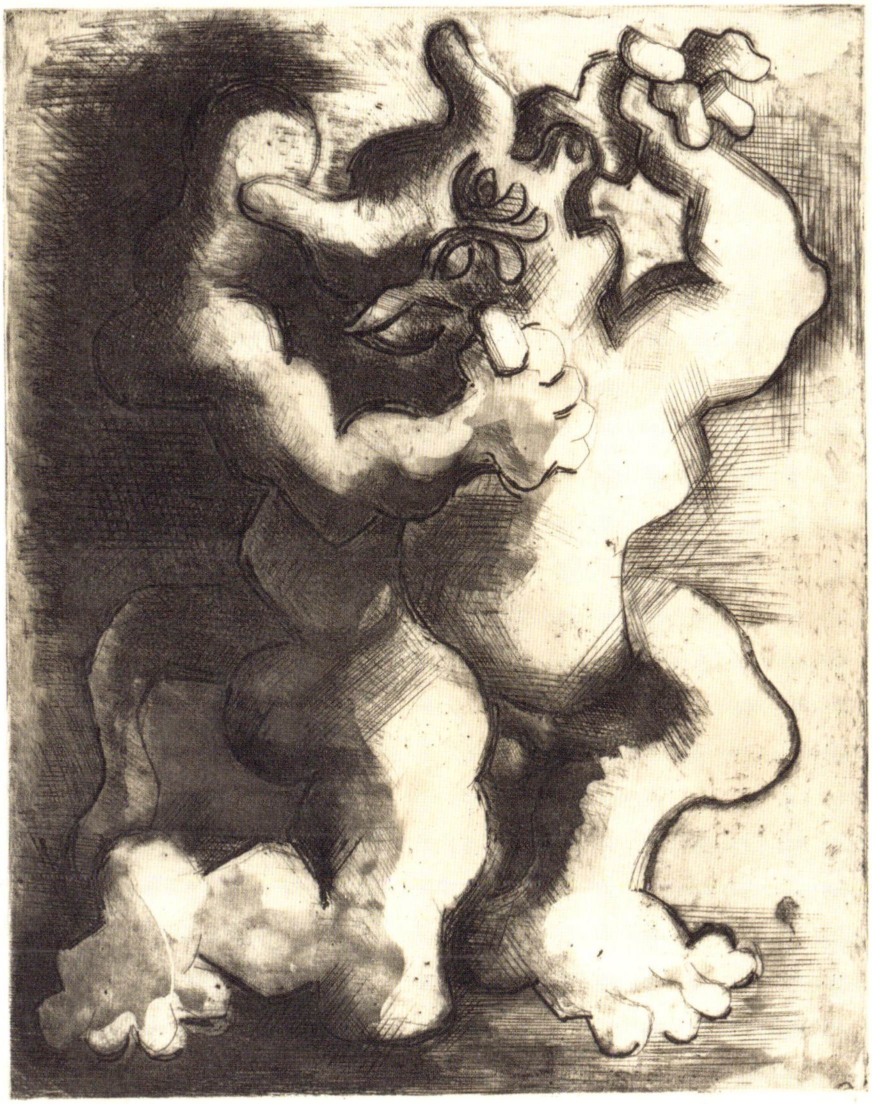

28/50

Cat. 8

JACQUES LIPCHITZ
(Druskininkai, 1891 – Capri, 1973)
The Road to Exile, 1944
Etching and aquatint on paper, 513 × 331 mm
Signed l. r.: Lipchitz; l. l.: 32/33
Private collection

Drawing played a key role throughout Lipchitz's career, although he never saw his drawings as autonomous works, but as preparatory studies for his sculpture. After emigrating to America in 1941 he decided to consciously improve his skills in printmaking techniques, probably due to interest in prints among collectors, as well as the limited financial opportunities during wartime. His experimental works were produced in collaboration with the legendary Atelier 17 studio, which relocated from Paris to New York in the war years, led by Stanley William Hayter (1901–1988), who had previously worked with surrealist artists. The piece entitled *The Road to Exile*, reflecting on his personal experiences, was made a few years after his arrival in the USA. This dramatic composition of figures clinging tightly to each other, built on powerful contrasts of light and shade, is among the rare works on paper in his œuvre that were never turned into sculpture. This print and his countless drawings on this theme were regarded by Lipchitz as so well "resolved" that it was not worth elaborating the motif into sculpture.

[DS]

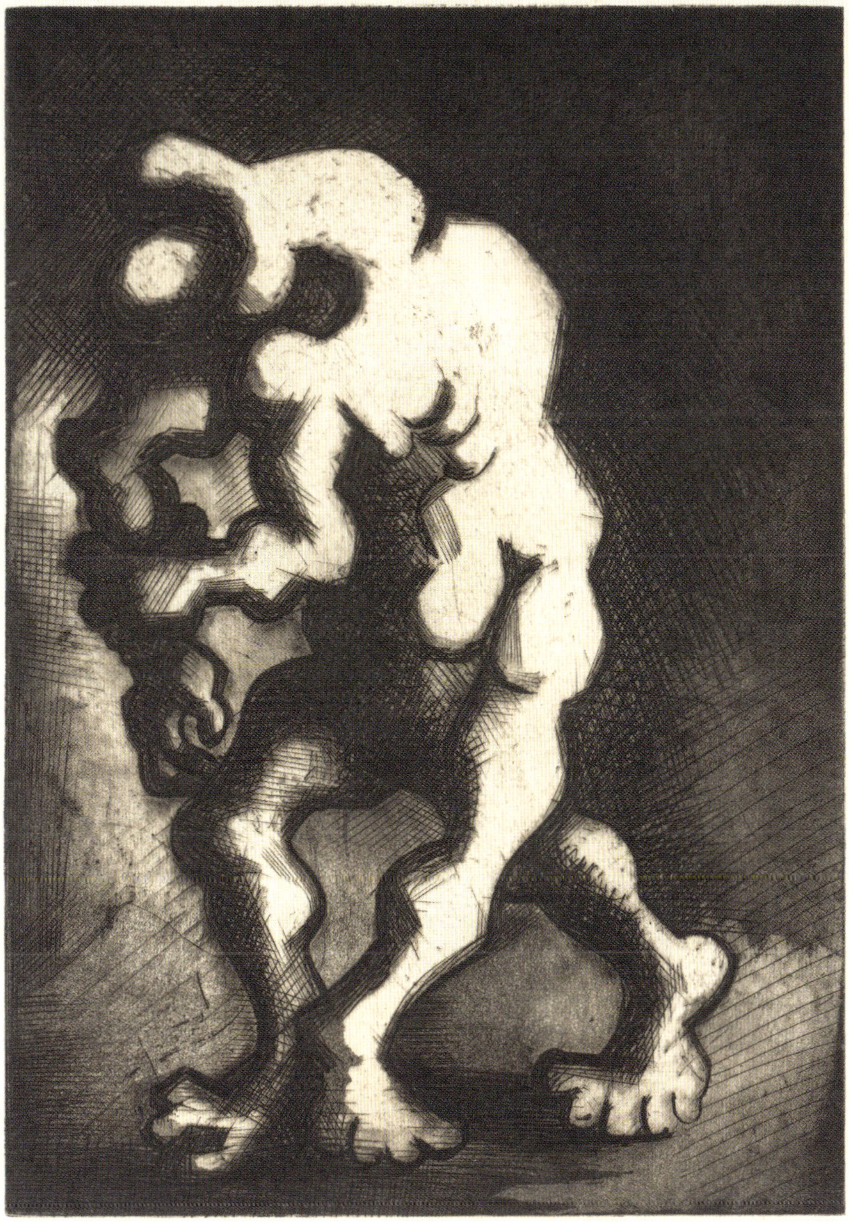

32/33

Cat. 9

JACQUES LIPCHITZ

(Druskininkai, 1891 – Capri, 1973)

Pages from the portfolio: *The Drawings of Jacques Lipchitz* (New York: Curt Valentin, 1944)

Collotype prints, 380 × 280 mm

Private collection

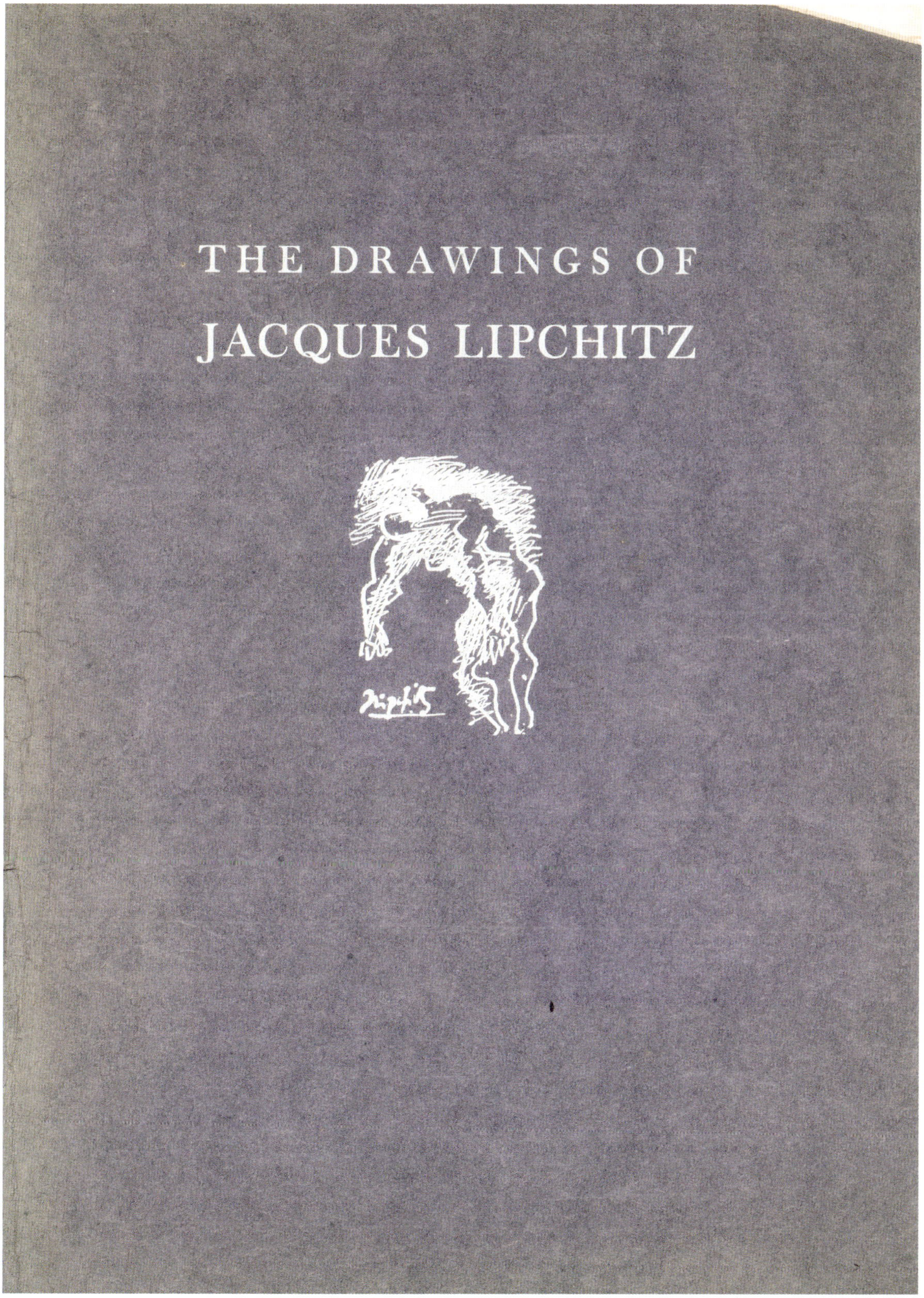

THE DRAWINGS OF
JACQUES LIPCHITZ

THE DRAWINGS OF
JACQUES LIPCHITZ

NEW YORK · 1944
CURT VALENTIN

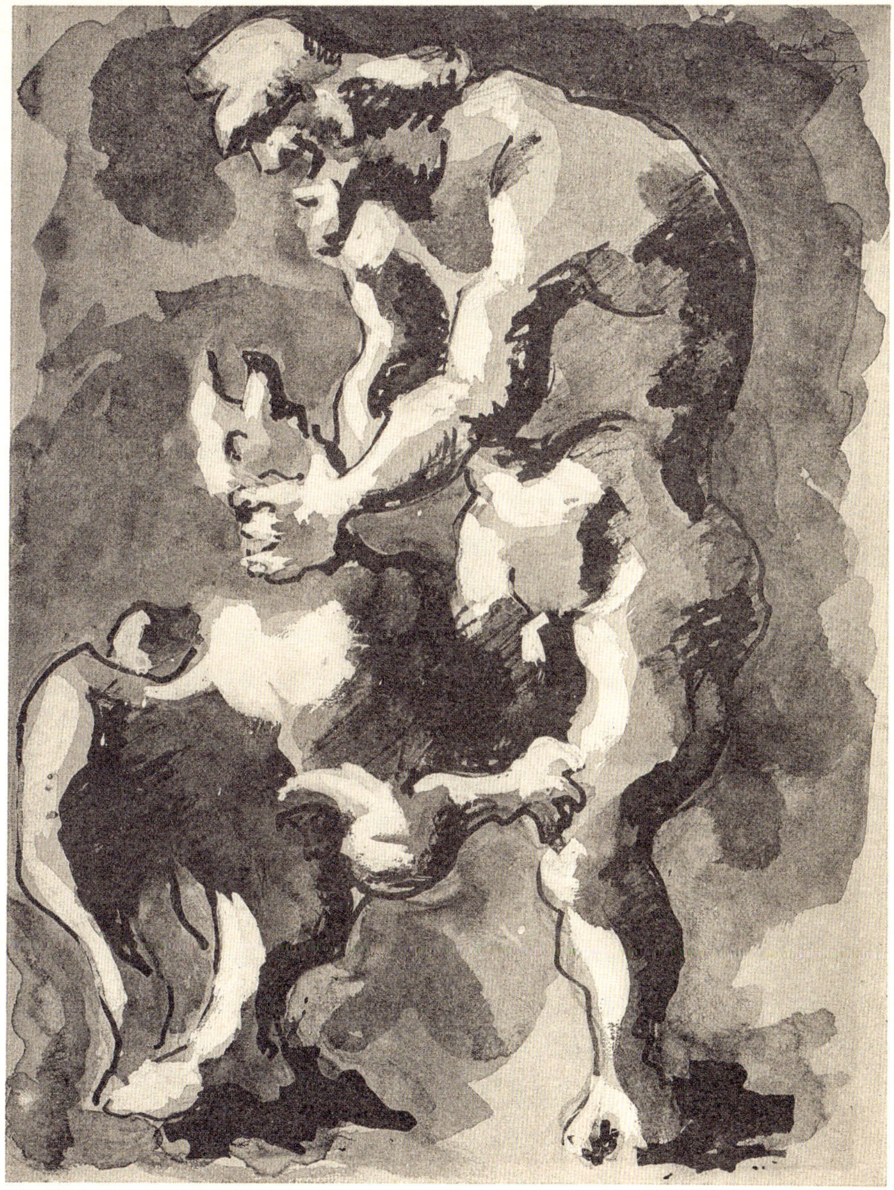

Prometheus

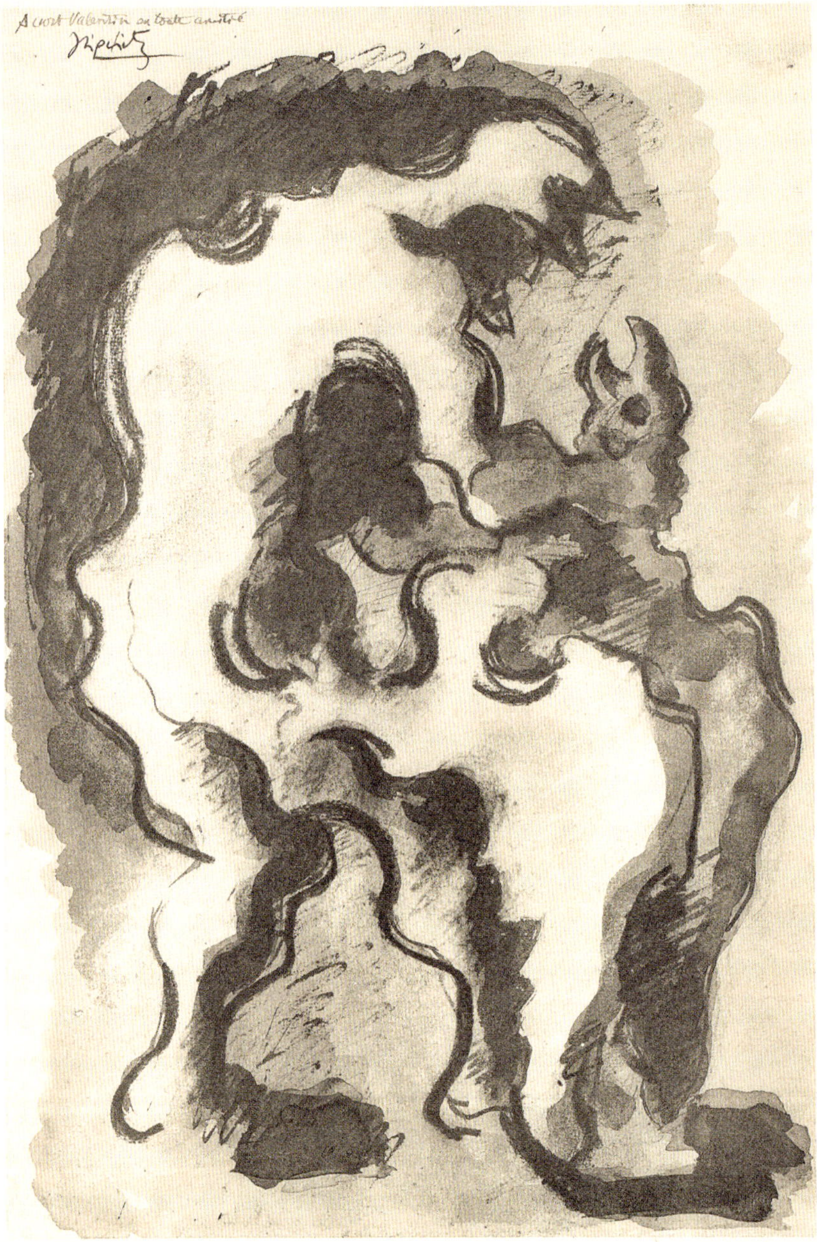

2

Prometheus

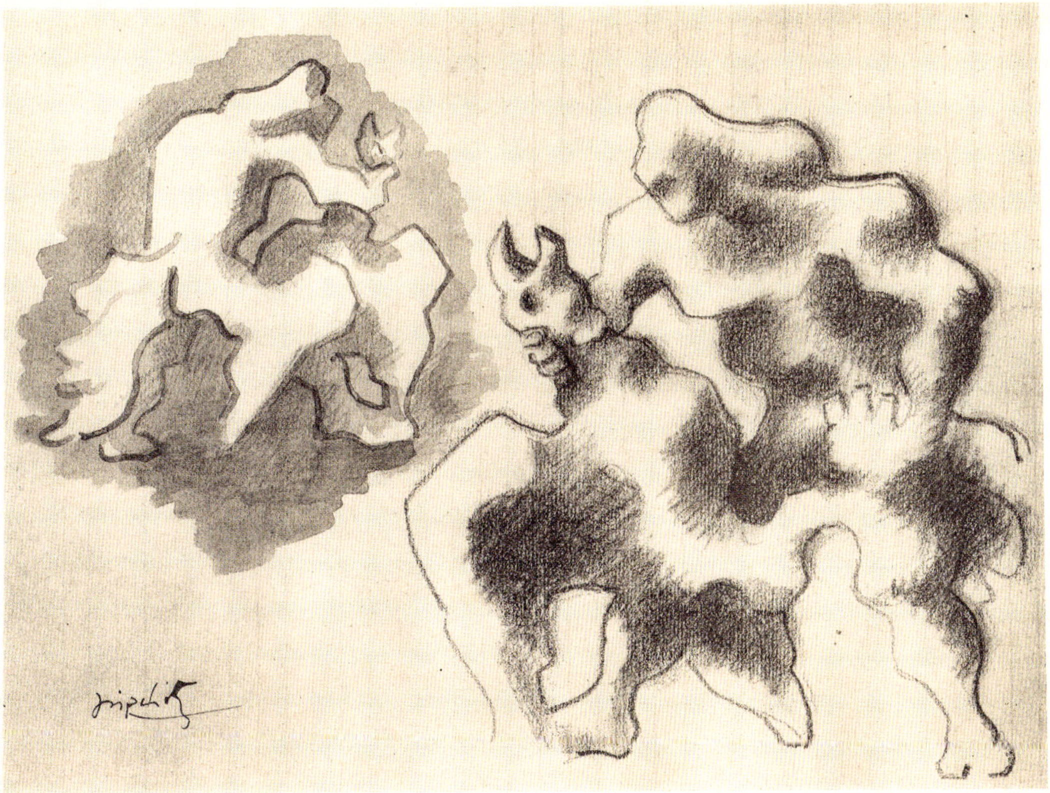

3

Prometheus

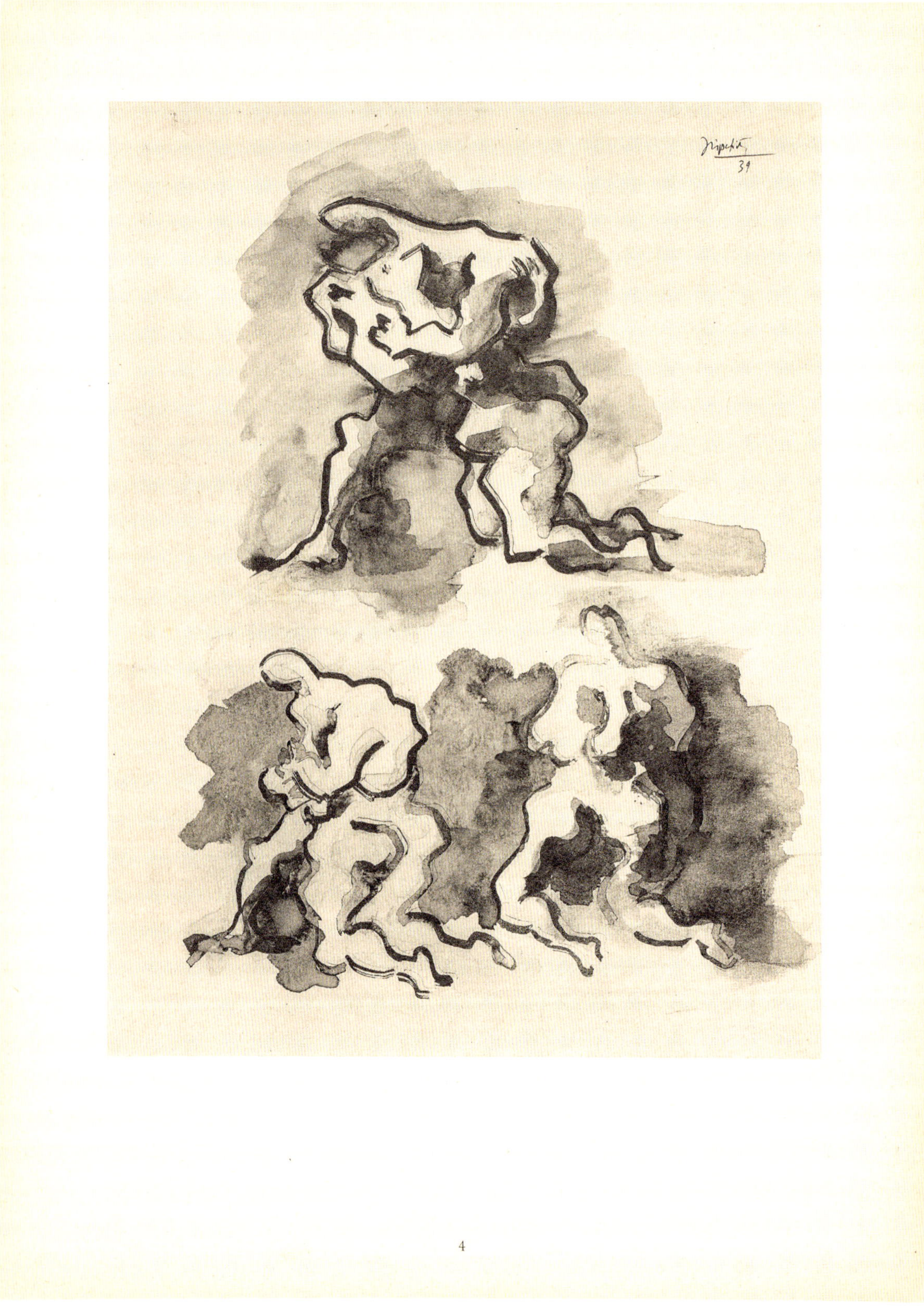

4

Couple

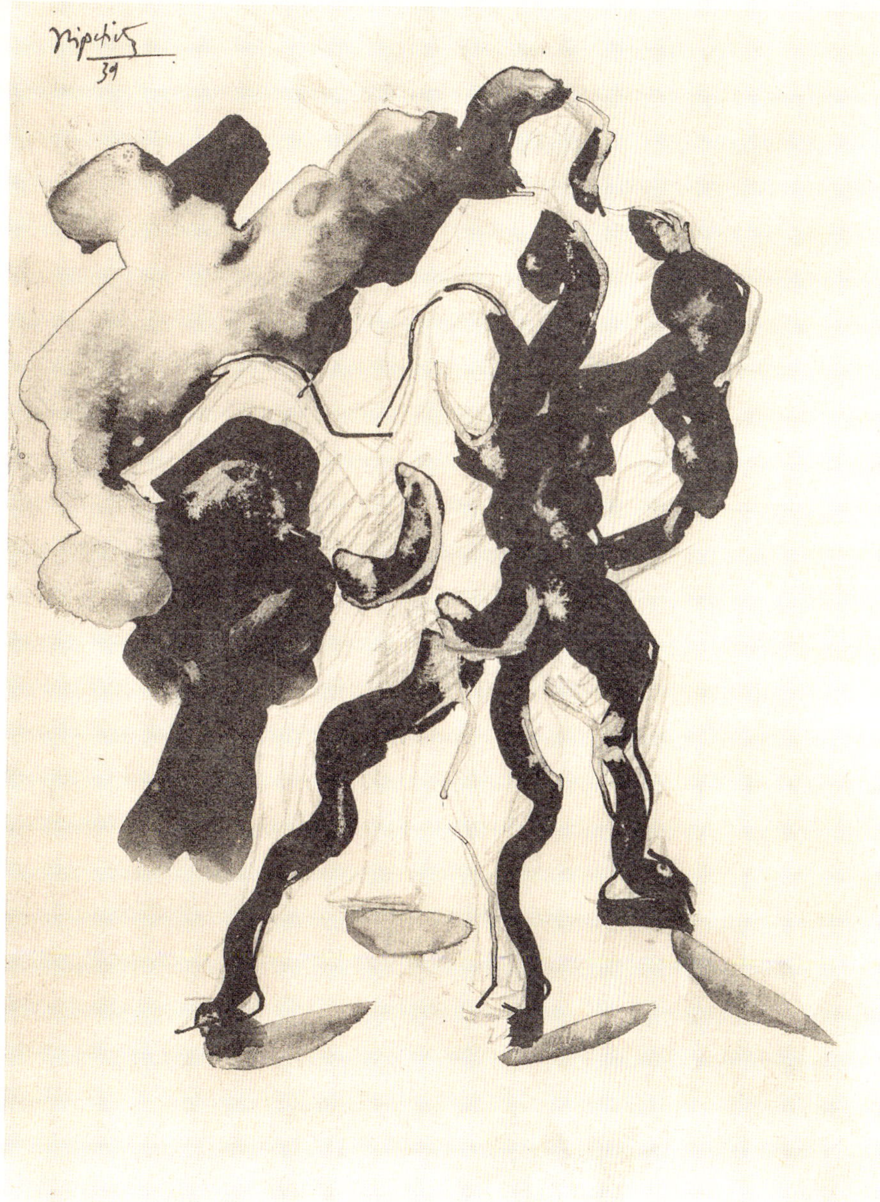

5

Rescue

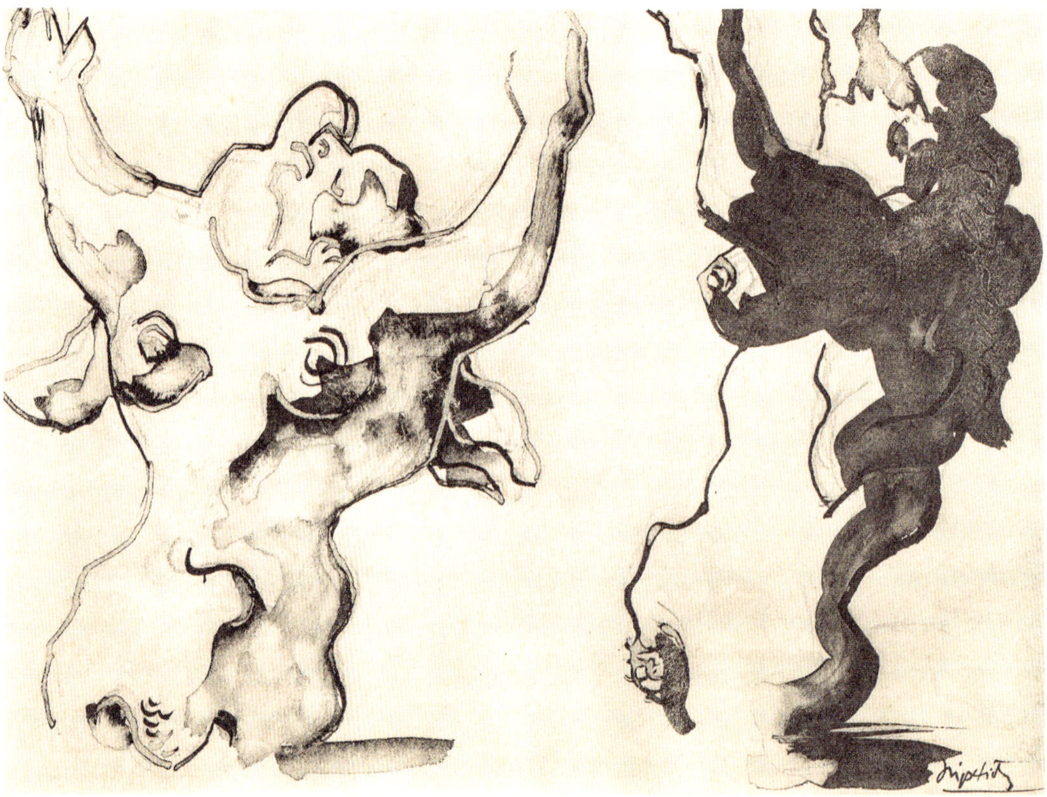

6

Mother and Child

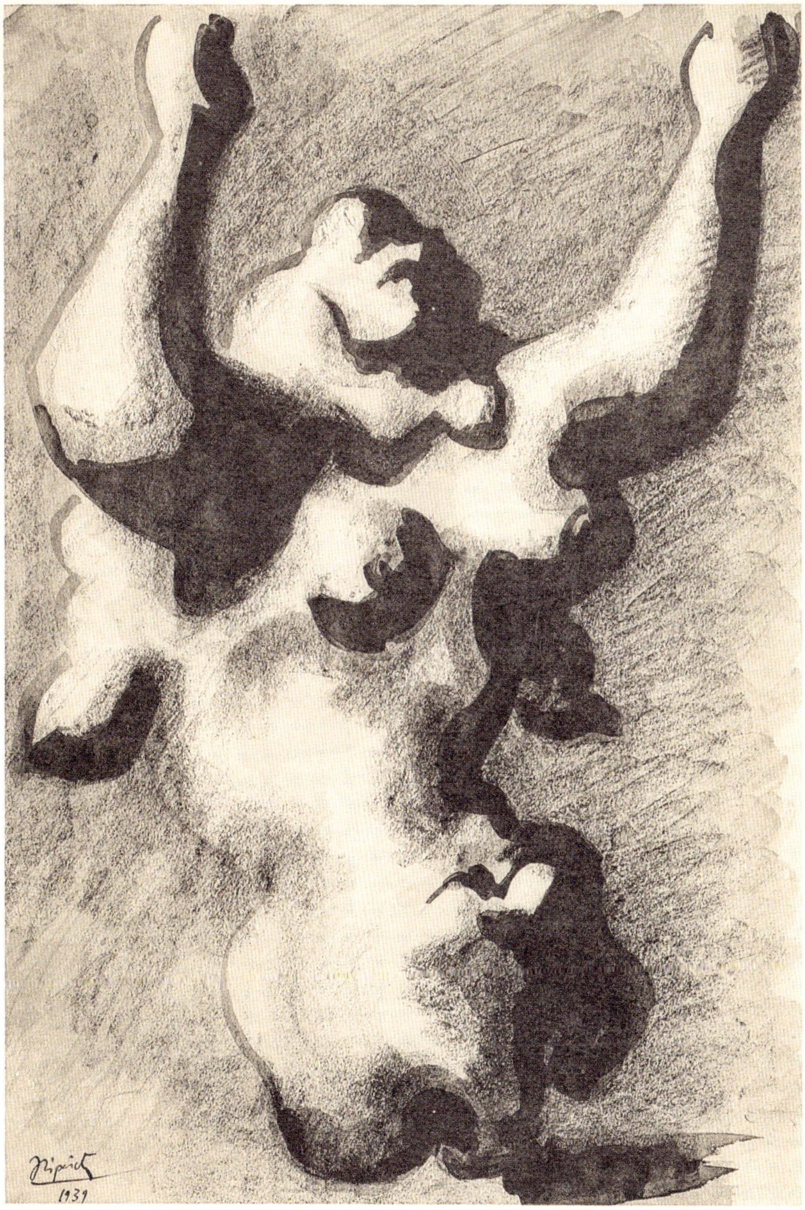

7

Study for
Mother and Child

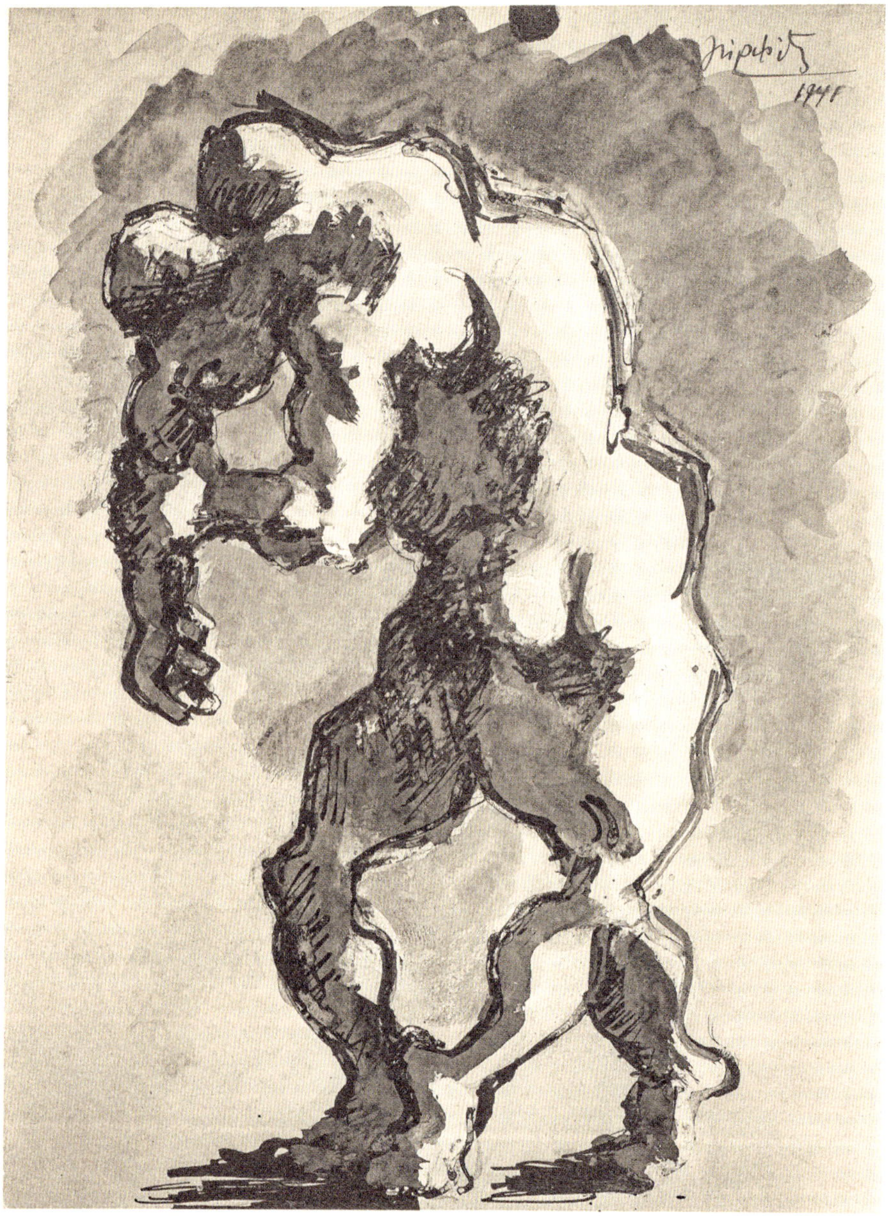

8

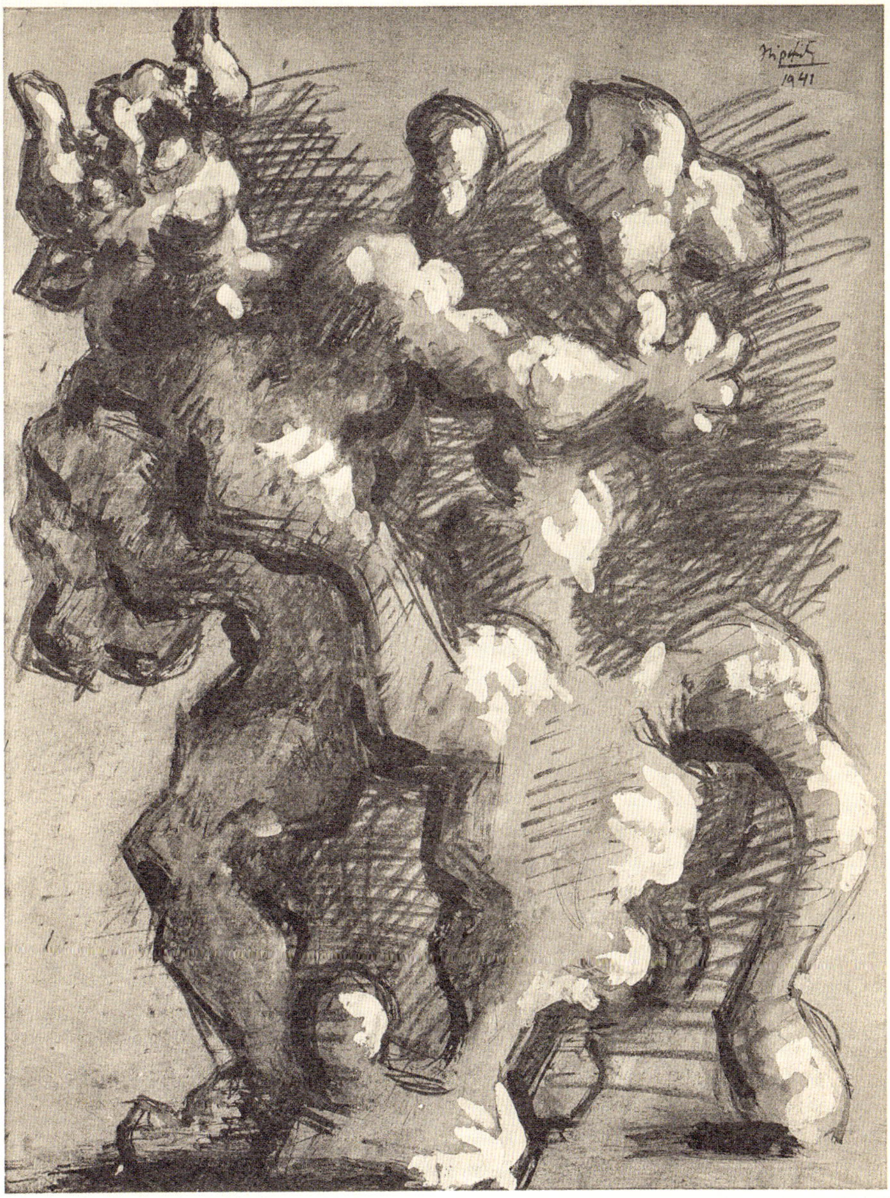

9

The Rape of Europa

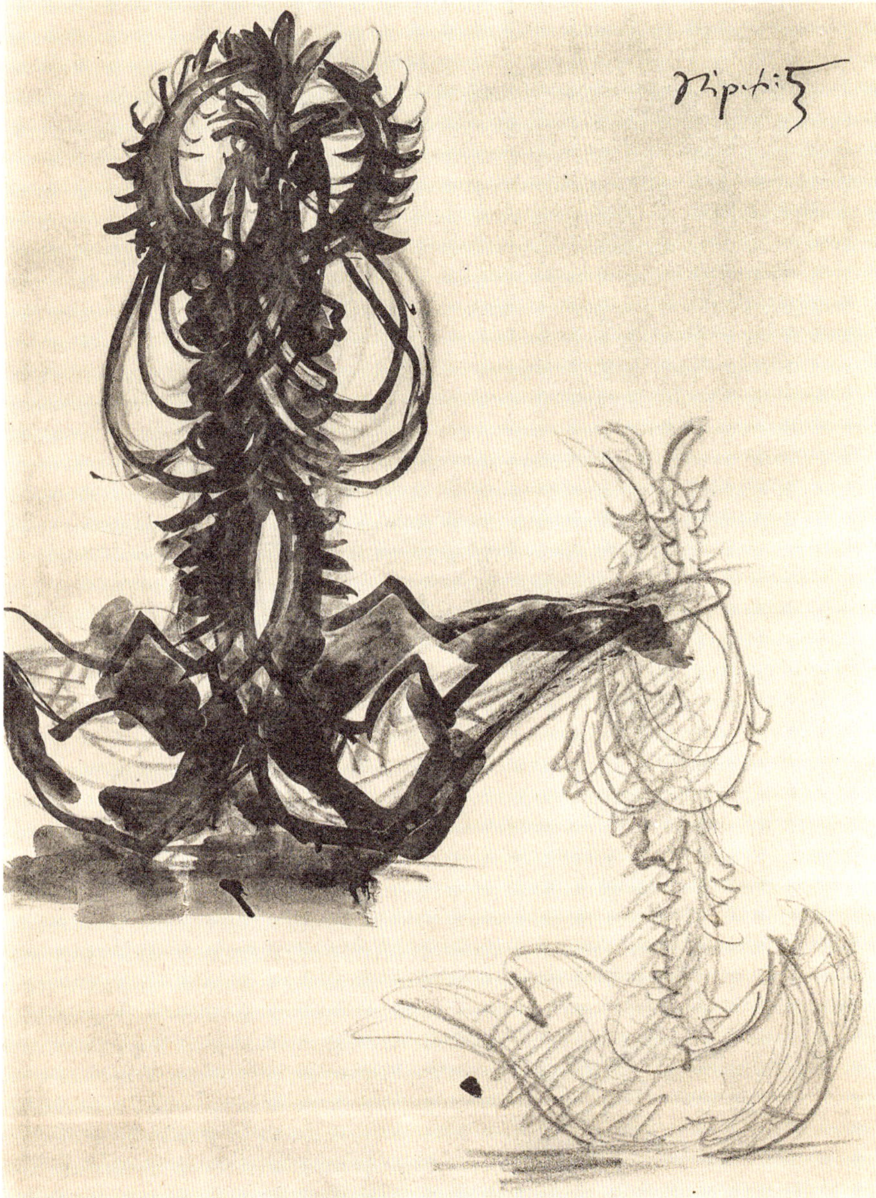

10

Yara

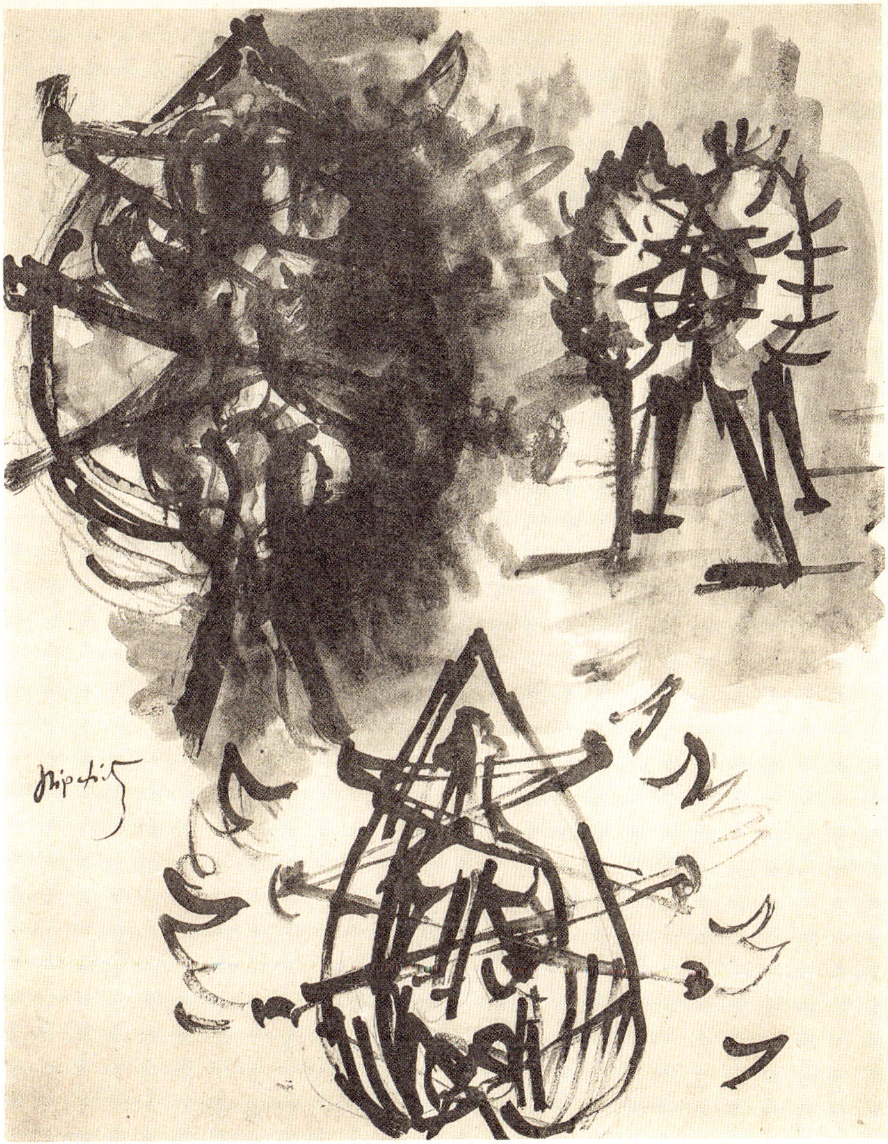

II

Spring

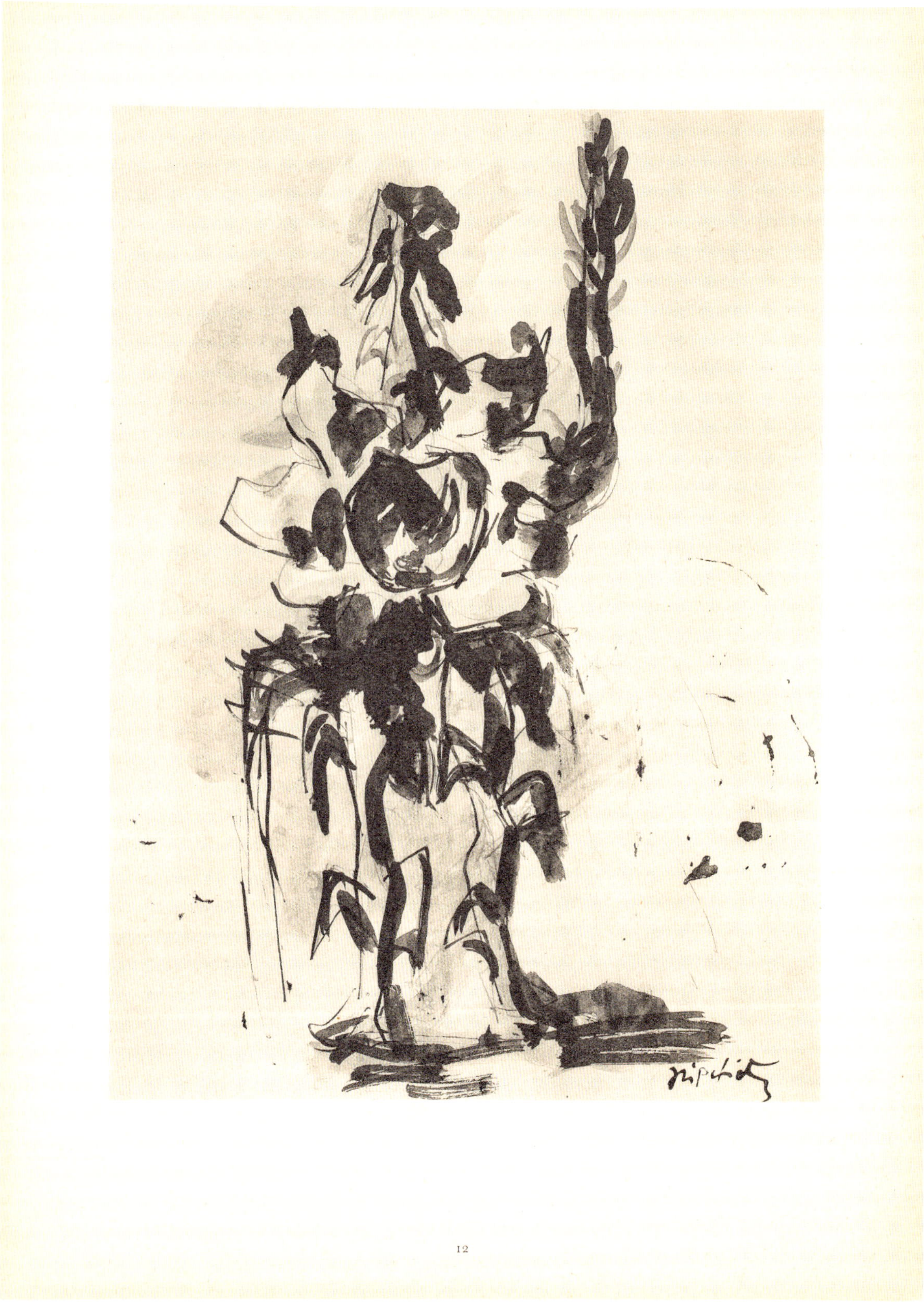

Pilgrim

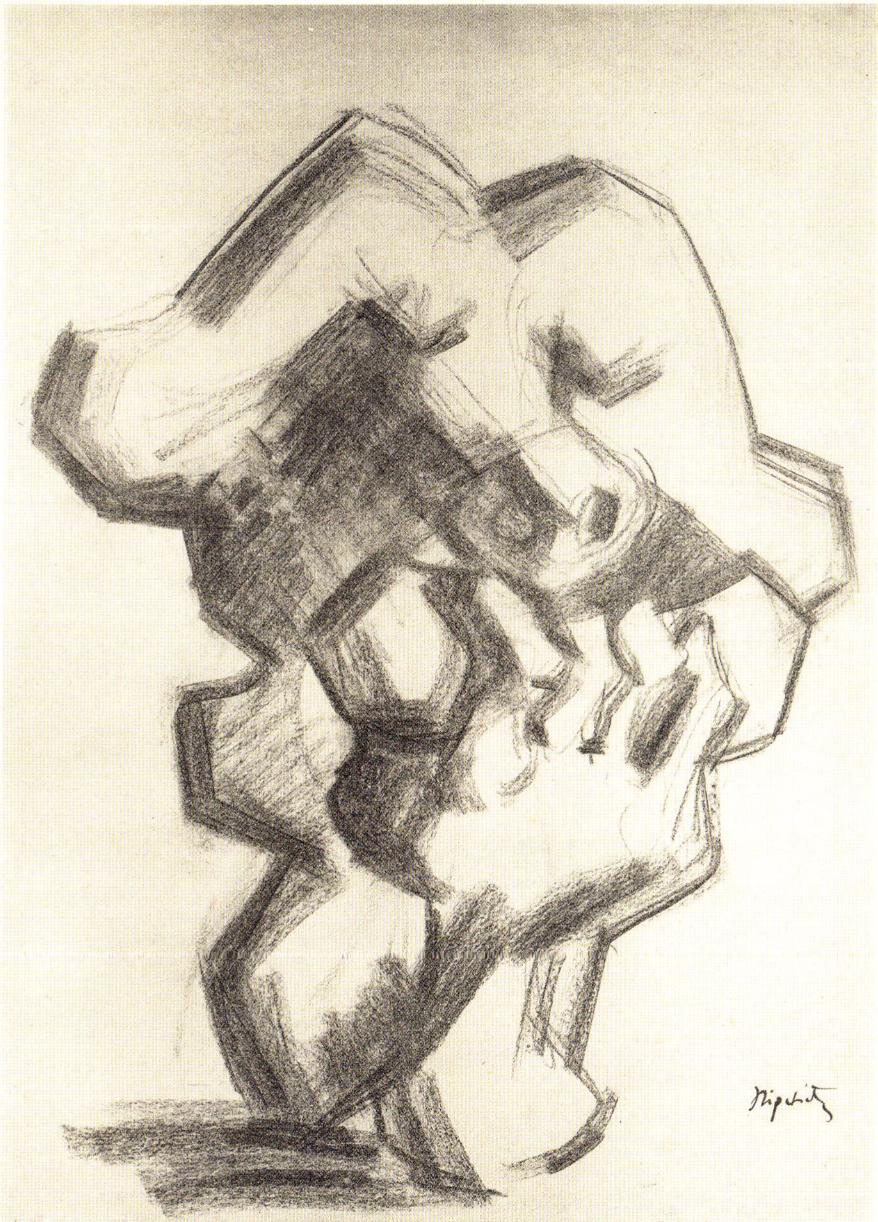

13

Pastoral

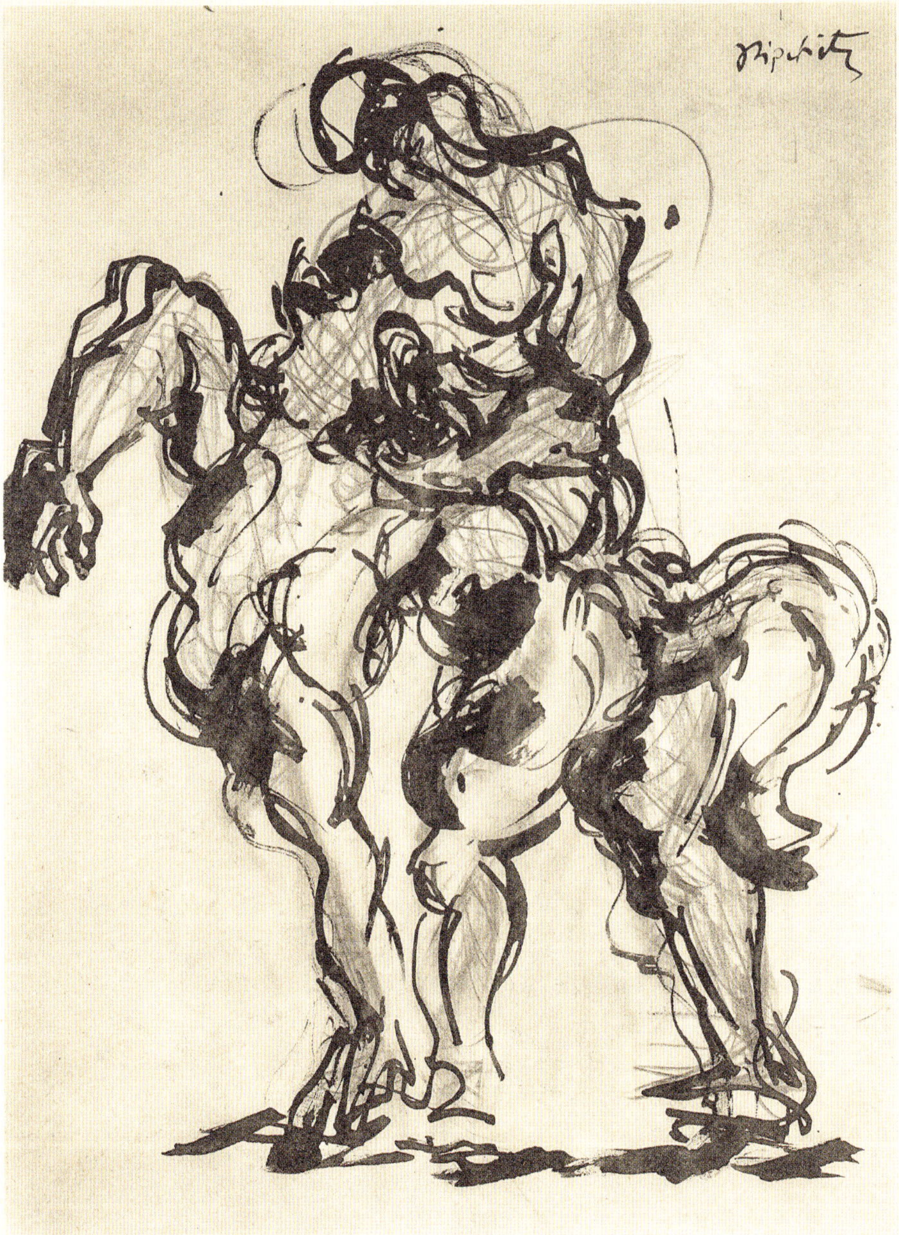

14

Theseus

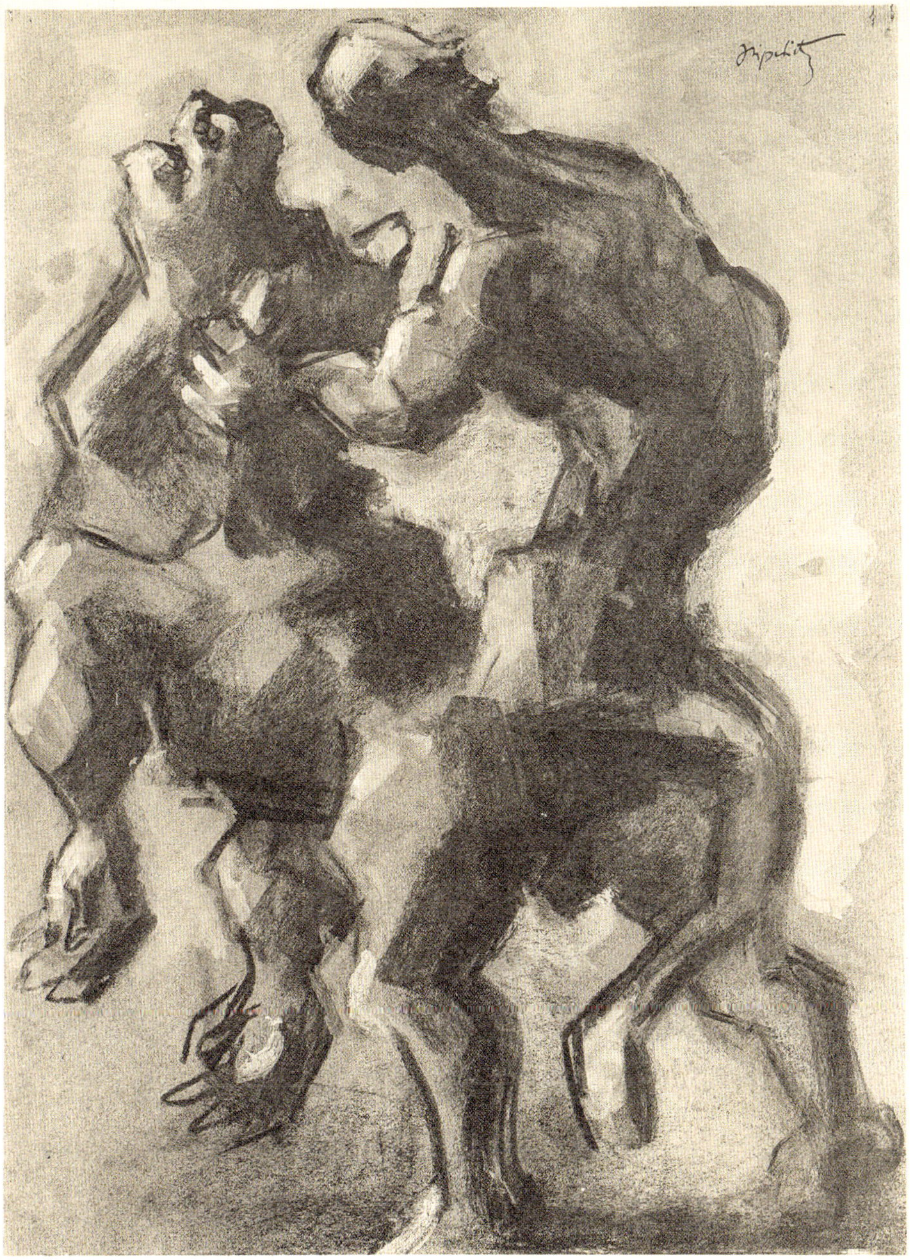

15

Theseus

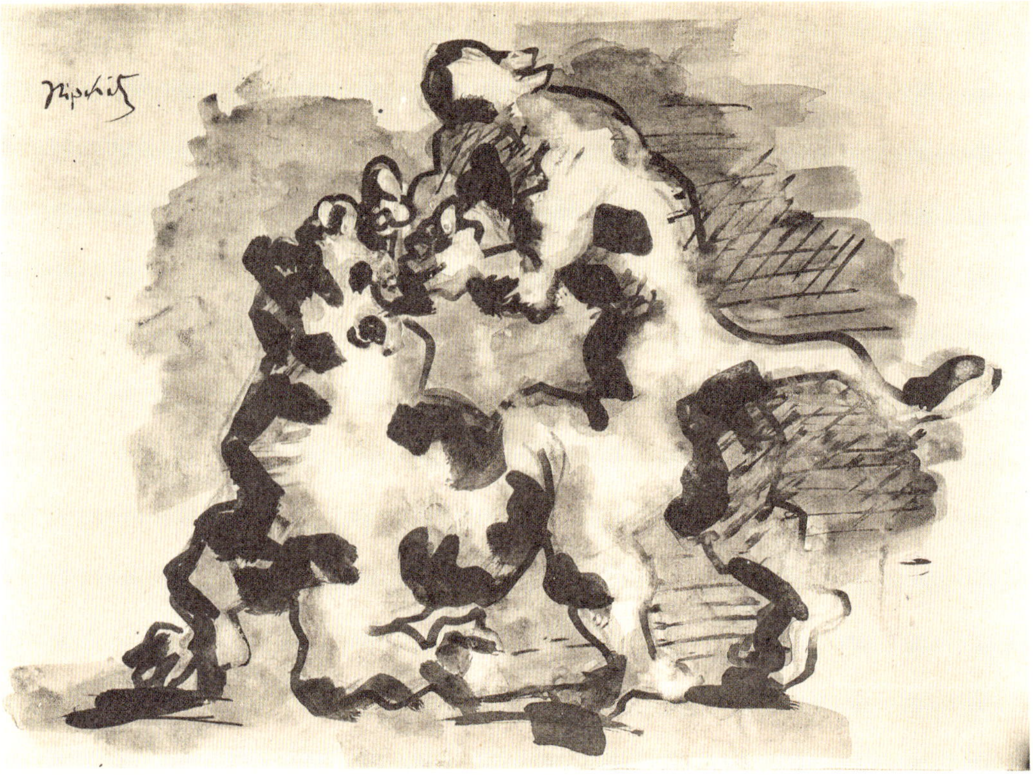

16

Theseus

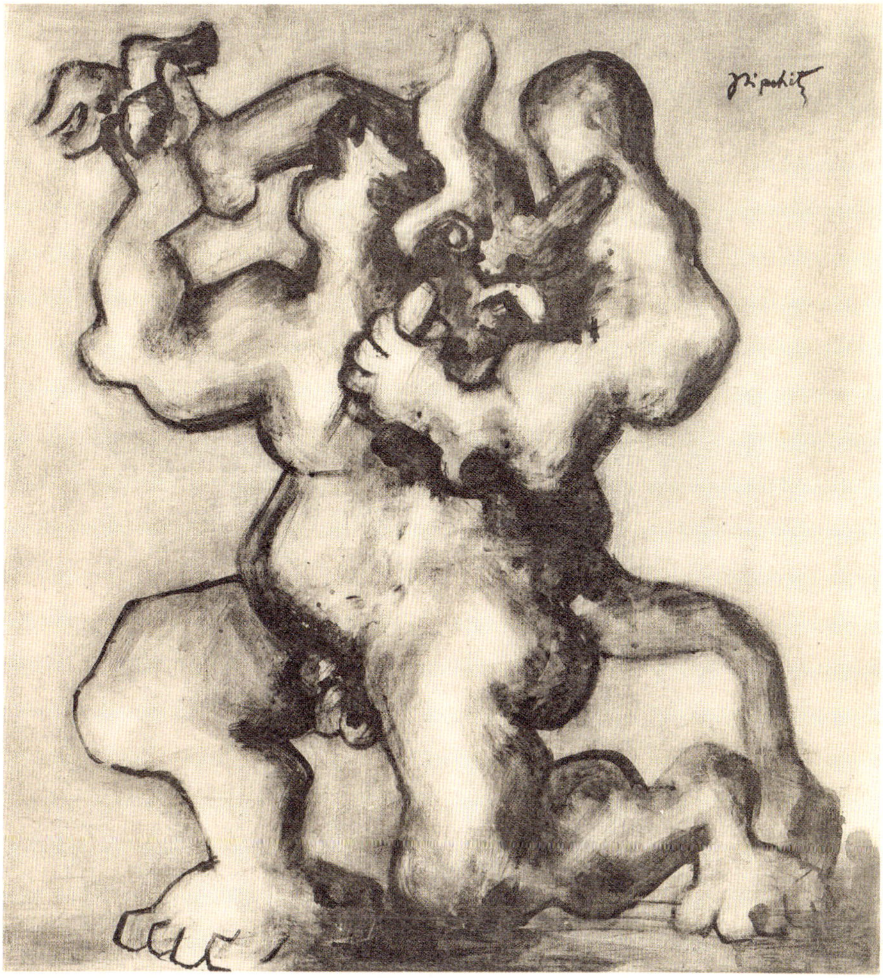

18

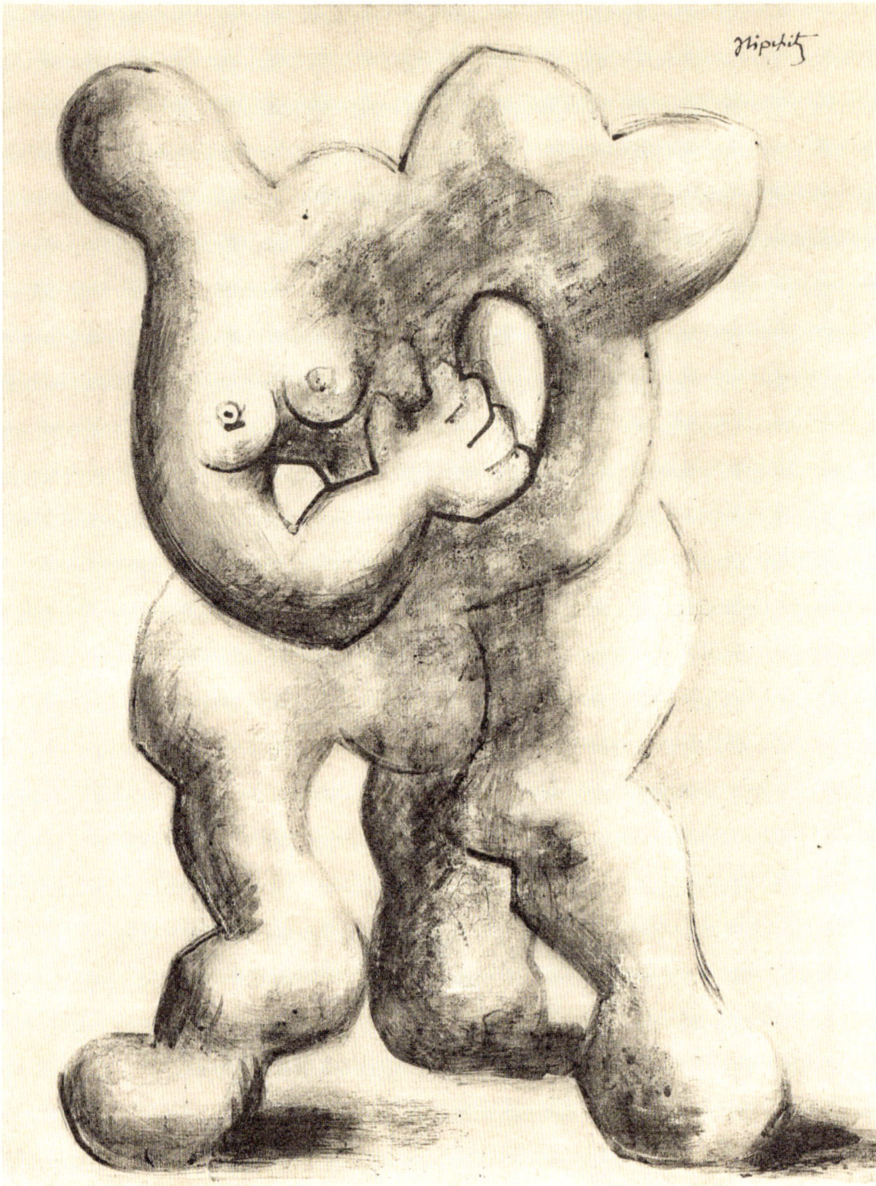

19

Benediction

CURT VALENTIN · NEW YORK

Cat. 10

JACQUES LIPCHITZ
(Druskininkai, 1891 – Capri, 1973)
Nude and Cock, 1945
Aquatint and drypoint on paper, 306 × 230 mm
Signed l. r.: Lipchitz; l. l.: 10/50
Private collection

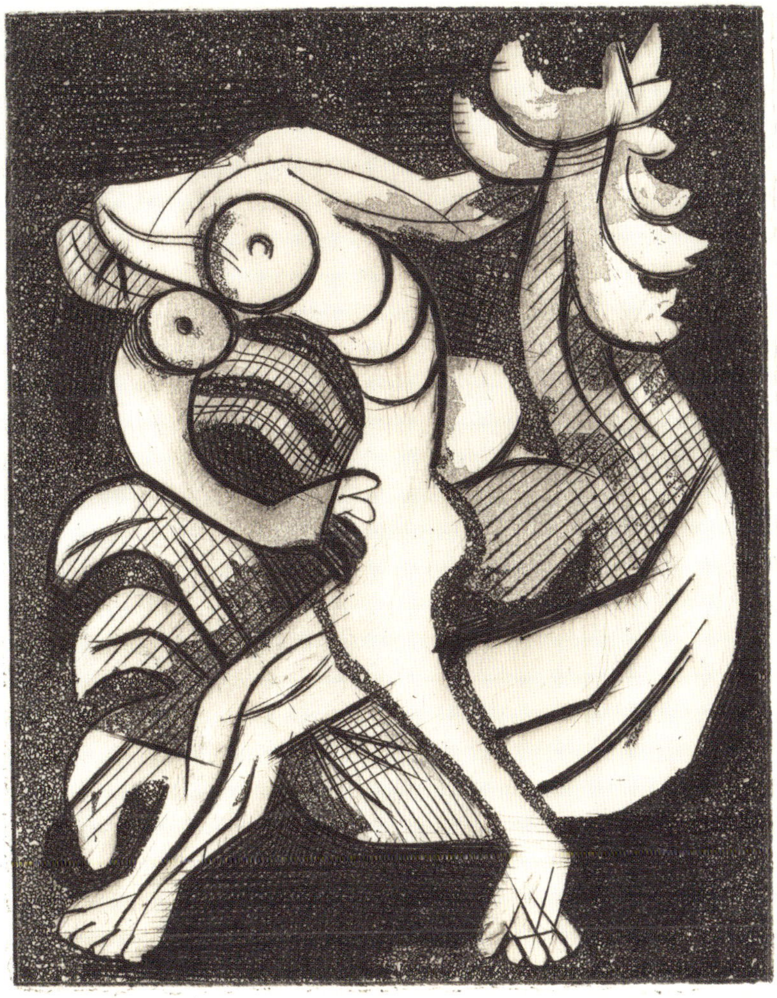

Cat. 11

[Cat. 12] page 92–93

AMÉDÉE OZENFANT
(Saint-Quentin, 1886 – Cannes, 1966)
Harmonics, ca. 1960
Lithograph on paper, 1044 × 744 mm
Signed l. r.: Ozenfant 41/110
Private collection

In spirit, Amédée Ozenfant's art was both reaction and counterreaction to that of his contemporary, Pablo Picasso, while in form it can be associated with the works of Juan Gris and Jacques Lipchitz. Raised in a well-off bourgeois family in northern France, by the time Ozenfant encountered the contemporary trends in Paris, he was already impassioned with the art of Nicolas Poussin (1594–1665), Jean Auguste Dominique Ingres (1780–1867), Georges Seurat (1780–1867) and Paul Cezanne. This was the common ground that led him into the social and professional circles of Picasso, Max Jacob (1876–1944), Henri Matisse (1869–1954), and Lipchitz; he wrote regularly about their work in the avantgarde periodical *L'Elan*, founded in 1915 together with the poet Guillaume Apollinaire (1880–1918). In the cubist approach to form, Ozenfant found his own voice, which he refined in the spirit of purism, a movement formulated together with Charles-Édouard Jeanneret (aka Le Corbusier [1887–1965]), which they published in 1918 in a manifesto entitled *Après le Cubisme* (After Cubism). Their aim was to save cubism from what they condemned as its hollowness and self-serving ornamentality. In parallel with this — and almost concurrently with Picasso's classicist turn, reflecting on Ingres-esque traditions — Ozenfant, in pursuit of form at its most pure, began to produce compositions harnessing nothing but the power of the contour. Creating form with a single line, drawn dynamically with an assured hand, is a skill possessed by artists who can say very much with very little. Whether with a labyrinthine flow of lines or a single expressive arc, Ozenfant was capable, even in this reduced way, of conveying human figures in all their emotional richness.

[KB]

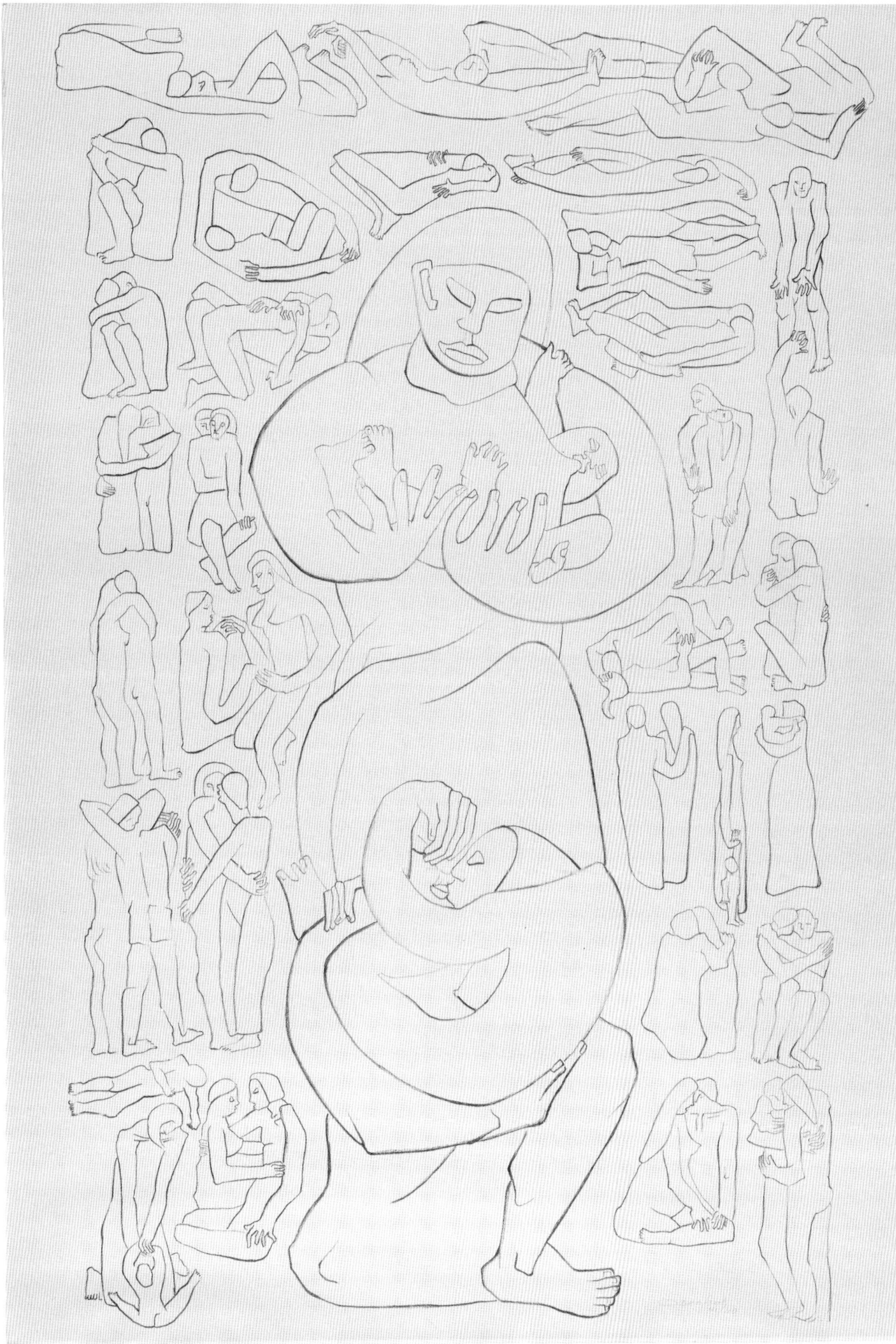

Cat. 12

AMÉDÉE OZENFANT
(Saint-Quentin, 1886 – Cannes, 1966)
Maternity II (Entwined Silhouettes), 1960
Lithograph on paper, 635 × 495 mm
Signed l. r.: Ozenfant 70/115
Museum of Fine Arts, Budapest, inv. no. L.85.48

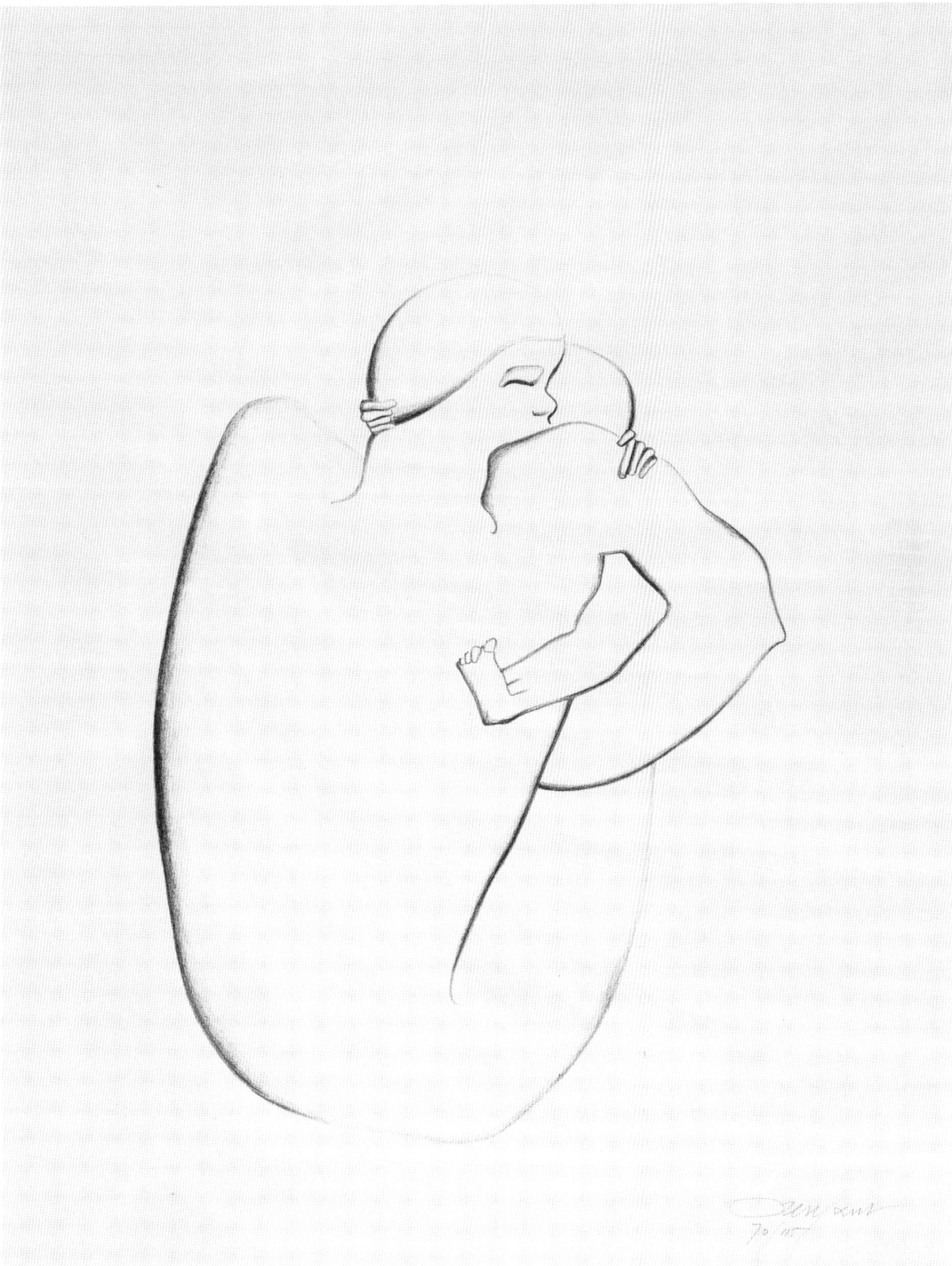

Cat. 13

[Cat. 14] page 96–97

JACQUES LIPCHITZ
(Druskininkai, 1891 – Capri, 1973)
Sketch for *Our Tree of Life*, version II, 1971–1972
Bronze, 23 × 15 × 8.5 cm
Cast: Fonderia Luigi Tommasi, Pietrasanta
Signed: Lipchitz 4/7
Private collection
Wilkinson cat. 739

In 1947 Lipchitz was commissioned to produce a statue of the Virgin Mary for the church of Notre-Dame-de-Toute-Grâce in Assy, France. He was delighted at this request, and around the same time it occurred to him to craft a memorial to the Jewish faith as well: "When I had started to make the Virgin in 1947, I immediately had ideas about doing something similar related to my own religion."[1] Over the years, he made numerous preparatory sketches and maquettes on the theme, many of which were destroyed in a fire at the sculptor's New York studio in 1952. In the 1960s he began to focus on the project once more, having received a commission from the Hadassah University Hospital of Jerusalem to create a monumental memorial, and he started to develop and expand his earlier ideas in preparation for the new sculpture. In terms of structure, the work is similar to his Virgin in Assy, entitled *Notre-Dame-de-Liesse* and completed in 1962, while in composition it resembles a tree, whose trunk and branches depict the main episodes and elements in the history of Judaism: Noah; Abraham's sacrifice of Isaac, interrupted by an angel; the Three Patriarchs; Moses and the Burning Bush, kneeling before the Tablets of the Law. The drama, tension and dynamism of the composition is augmented by the interweaving of the figures. The majority of the small bronze maquettes, including these preparatory studies from the private collection, are works filled with vitality and freshness. The final version of *Our Tree of Life* was erected on Mount Scopus in Jerusalem and unveiled in 1978, five years after the artist's death; work on the sculpture was overseen by Lipchitz's widow, Yulla.

[AS]

1 Jacques Lipchitz and H. Harvard Arnason, *My Life in Sculpture* (New York: The Viking Press, 1972), 198.

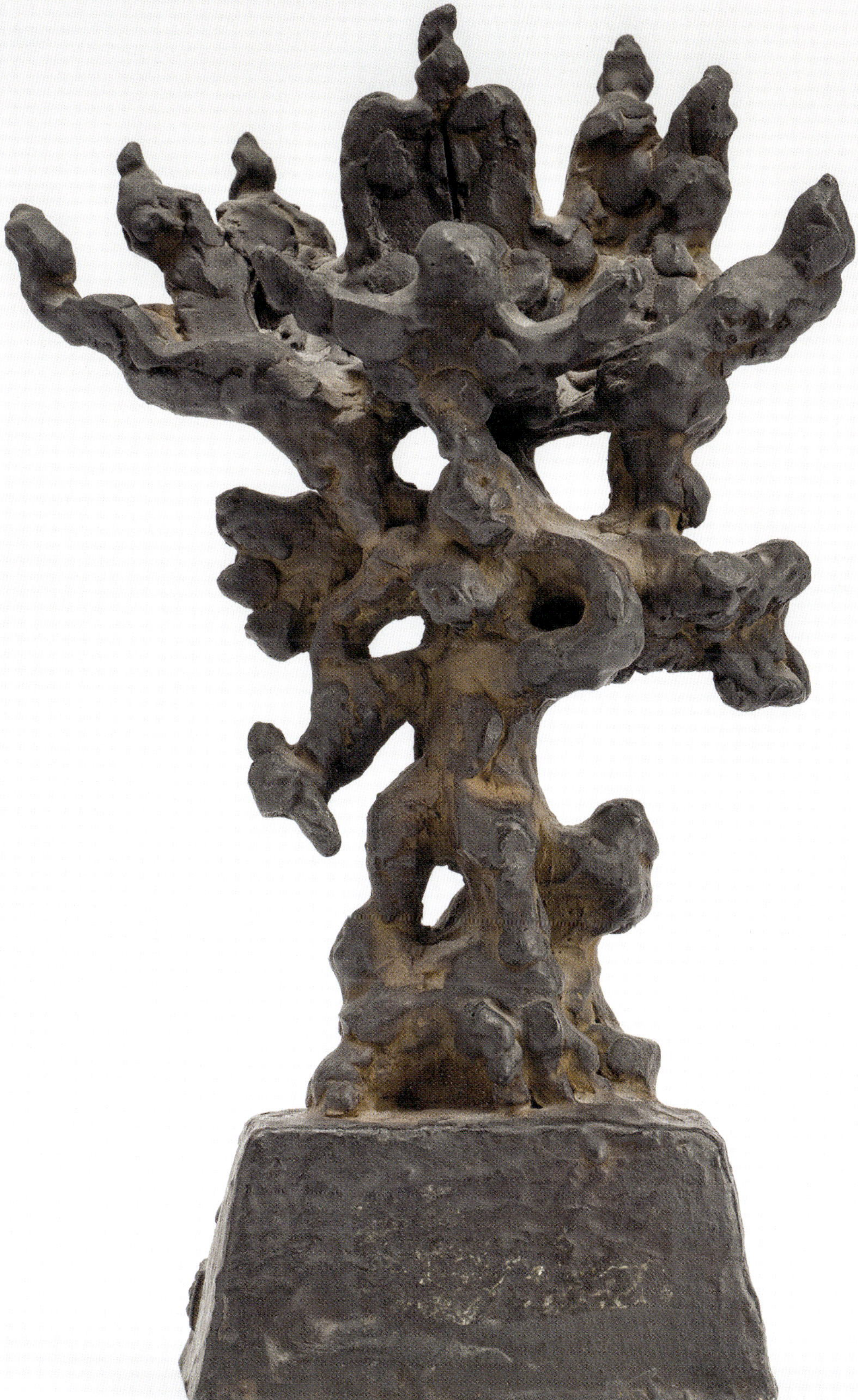

Cat. 14

JACQUES LIPCHITZ
(Druskininkai, 1891 – Capri, 1973)
Sketch for *Our Tree of Life*, version IV, 1971–1972
Bronze, 47 × 15.5 × 11.5 cm
Signed: Lipchitz 6/7
Private collection
Wilkinson cat. 741

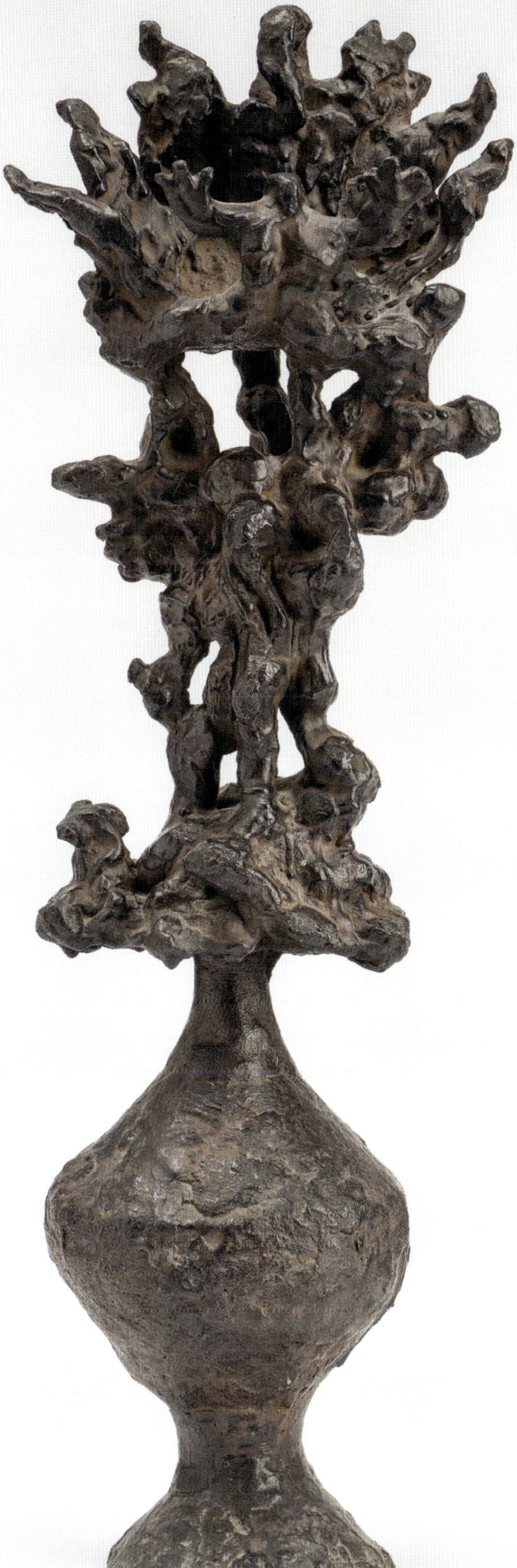

Cat. 15

ARBIT BLATAS
(Kaunas, 1908 – New York, 1999)
Portrait of Jacques Lipchitz, 1962
Lithograph on paper, 498 × 326 mm
Private collection

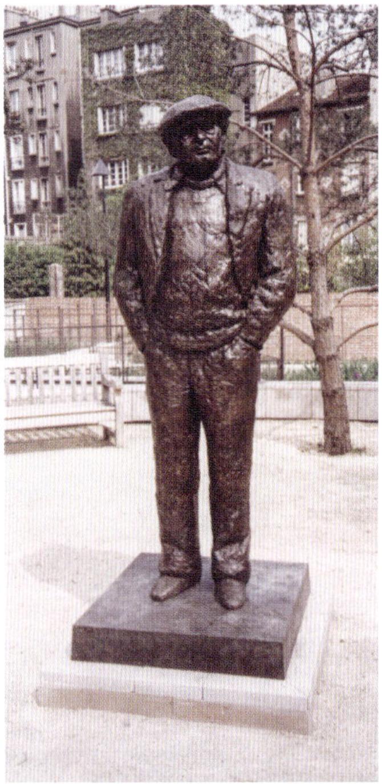

17 Arbit Blatas
Statue of Jacques Lipchitz, 1991
Garden of the Town Hall,
Boulogne-Billancourt

As one of the youngest members of the École de Paris, Arbit Blatas used paper, canvas and bronze to immortalise many of the defining artists of the early twentieth century. While Blatas was seventeen years younger than Lipchitz, their lives followed similar paths. Both were born in Lithuania, both moved to Paris, the art capital of the world, in their youth, and they both emigrated to the USA in 1941. In their new home, they often met up and reminisced about the places of their childhoods and their time in Montparnasse. Blatas produced a number of portraits of Lipchitz between 1962 and 1964. The lithograph on show here stems from this period, and it was published in New York in 1962 in the portfolio entitled *Homage à l'École de Paris*.[1] Besides that of Lipchitz, the album also contained lithographic portraits of other artists: Pierre Bonnard, Georges Braque, Marc Chagall, Raoul Dufy, Fernand Léger, Aristide Maillol, Albert Marquet, Henri Matisse, Pablo Picasso, Chaim Soutine, Maurice Utrillo, Maurice de Vlaminck and Édouard Vuillard. Years later, Blatas sculpted a full-length statue of Lipchitz, which in 1991 was erected in the garden of Boulogne-Billancourt Town Hall (fig. 17).

[AS]

1 *Homage à L'Ecole De Paris,* introduction by Emily Genauer (Paris: Editions Marcel Sautier; New York: Graphophile, 1962).

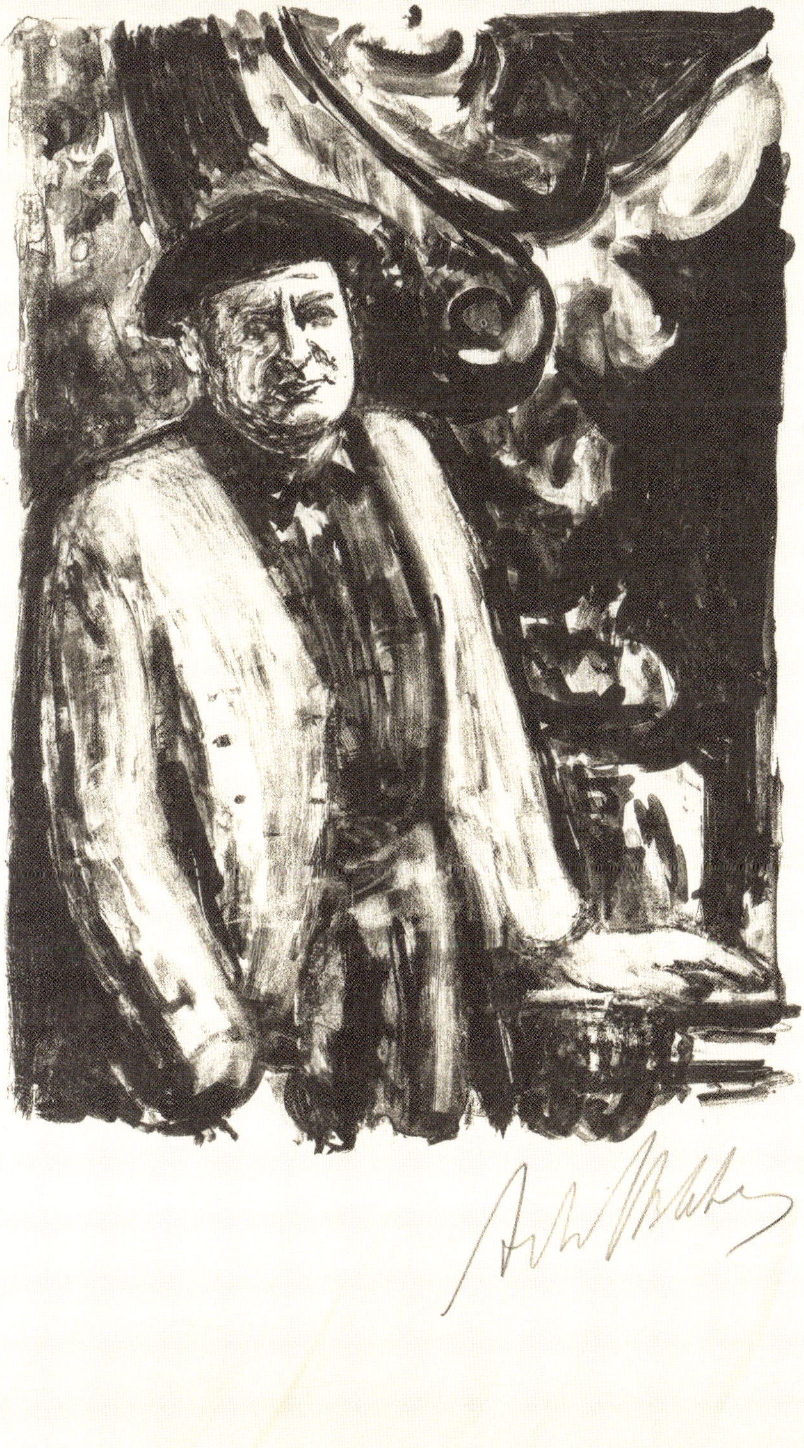

Cat. 16

[Cat. 17] page 102–103

JACQUES LIPCHITZ
(Druskininkai, 1891 – Capri, 1973)
Small study for *The Rape of Europa*, 1969–1970
Bronze, 13 × 11.2 × 7.5 cm
Private collection
Wilkinson cat. 681

The legend of Zeus transforming into a bull to abduct the nymph Europa is a recurring theme in Lipchitz's œuvre, its meaning constantly changing in line with the current situation. In works created in different periods, the expressive forms of the two figures, dynamically merging together, represent a passionate embrace at times, destruction and aggression at others. Lipchitz first tackled this ancient myth in 1938, when he emphasised the eroticism in the scene, following the classical iconographic tradition. During World War II, however, the artist viewed this well-known theme as a political and existential metaphor. In the sculptures and works on paper Lipchitz made in 1941, following his emigration to America, the bull is an embodiment of Hitler, while the nymph is a symbol of the invaded continent of Europe and the imperilment of Western culture. Here, Europa fends off her assailant with a dagger: as the artist later explained, the statue was intended as a "magical image"[1] through which he himself took up the fight against Nazism. Towards the end of his life, around 1969–1970, Lipchitz was once again intensely occupied by this story, producing a large number of sculpture studies and drawings, including the two works shown here.

[DS]

1 Jacques Lipchitz and H. Harvard Arnason, *My Life in Sculpture* (New York: The Viking Press, 1972), 159.

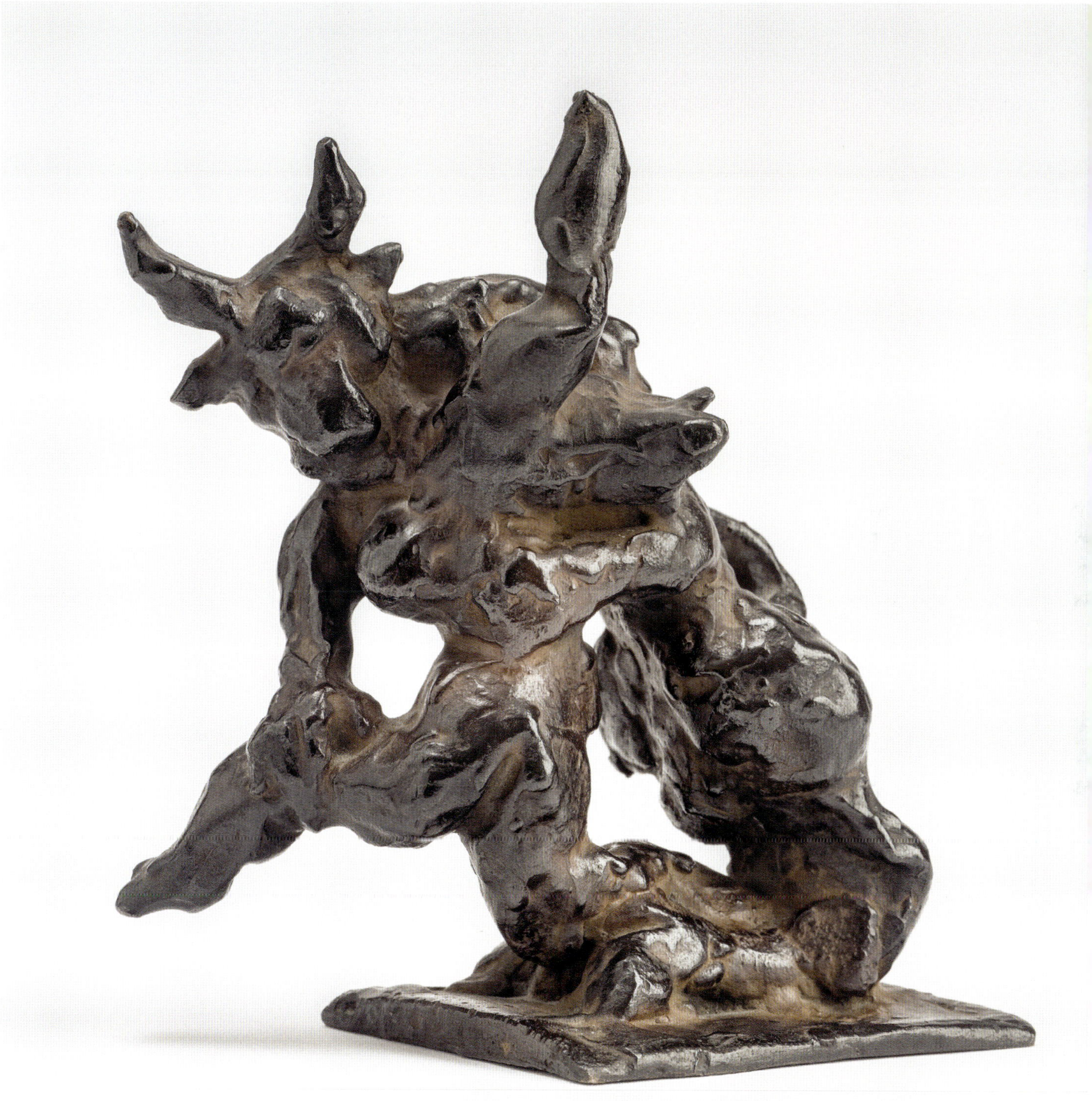

Cat. 17

JACQUES LIPCHITZ
(Druskininkai, 1891 – Capri, 1973)
The Rape of Europa, ca. 1970
Crayon on paper, 320 × 236 mm
Private collection

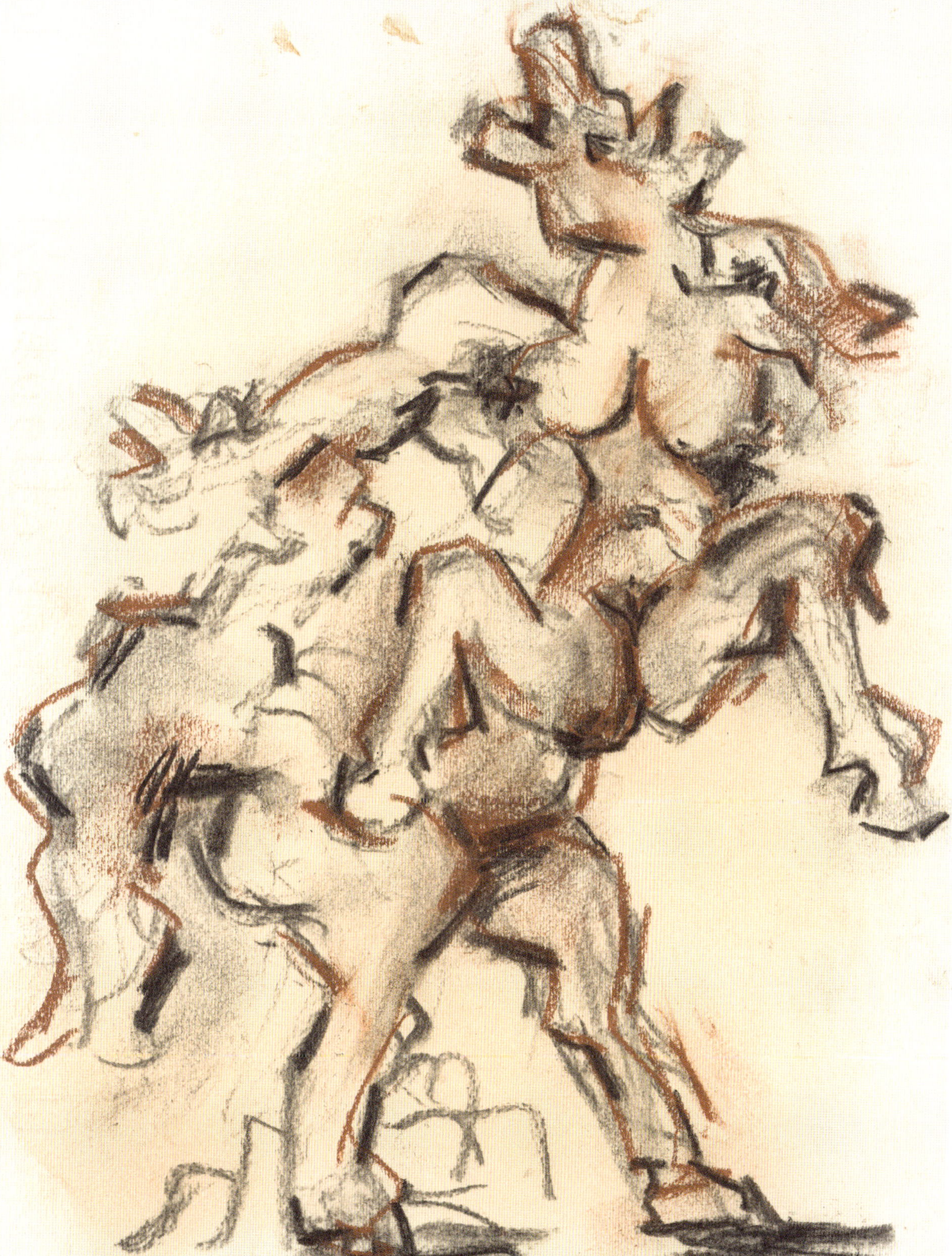

Cats. 18 and 19

JACQUES LIPCHITZ
(Druskininkai, 1891 – Capri, 1973)
Medallion with Self-Portrait (recto and verso), 1967
Bronze, diameter: 11 cm
Inscription: JACQUES LIPCHITZ SCULTORE 1967
Private collection

This relatively small bronze medallion — two copies of which feature in this exhibition — is unique in Lipchitz's œuvre. One side features a profile self-portrait of the elderly sculptor, depicted proudly with his characteristic flowing hair; Adina Kamien compares this dignified image to that of a Roman emperor.[1] On the other side, a young male nude kneels before a small block of stone, holding a hammer in his raised hand, a chisel in the other, presumably in the act of carving. Lipchitz made stone sculptures early on in his career, in the 1910s and 1920s, although he never truly took to working in stone, regarding it as too slow compared with modelling in clay. Whenever he could, he preferred to employ a professional mason to craft the stone in his stead. From the Italian inscription ("Jacques Lipchitz scultore", that is "Jacques Lipchitz sculptor") and the date (1967), it can be deduced that the medallion was made in Pietrasanta, Tuscany. The master discovered Italy in the early 1960s, and he subsequently spent every summer in Pietrasanta. By then, he had for decades made most of his sculptures using the lost-wax bronze casting method, and he chose this small Italian town mostly because of the famous foundry run by Luigi Tommasi; nevertheless, the proximity of Carrara and the centuries-old tradition of sculpture heavily influenced his idea of what sculpture and the sculptor should be, and he may for this reason have identified himself with the figure depicted on the medallion.

[AS]

1 Adina Kamien, "Jacques Lipchitz: Sculptural Encounters," see in this volume, 36.

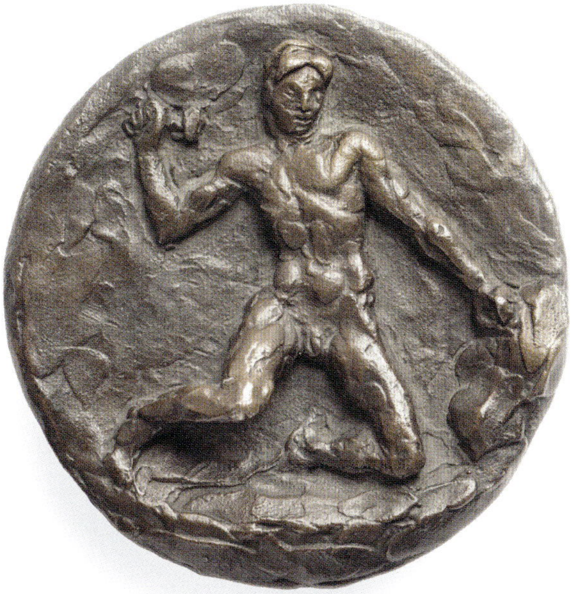

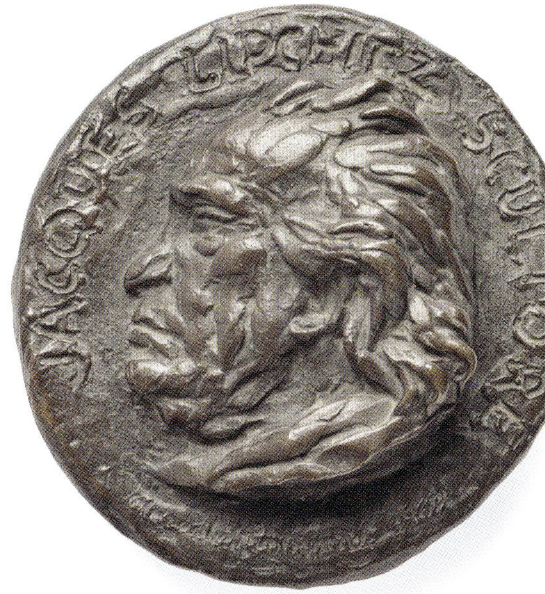
JACQUES LIPCHITZ SCULTORE

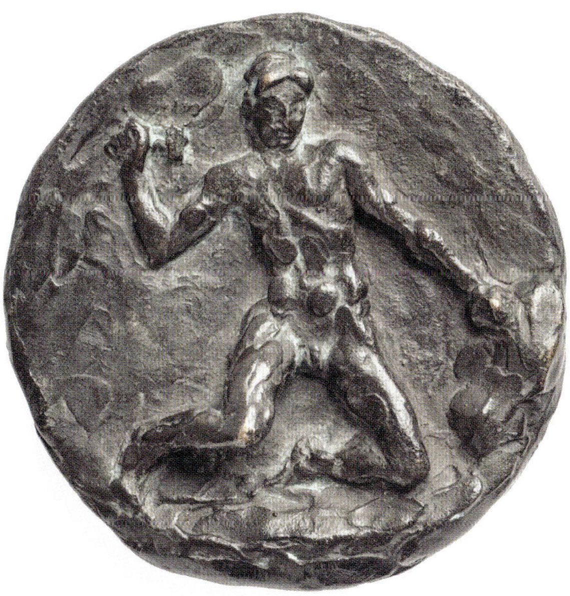

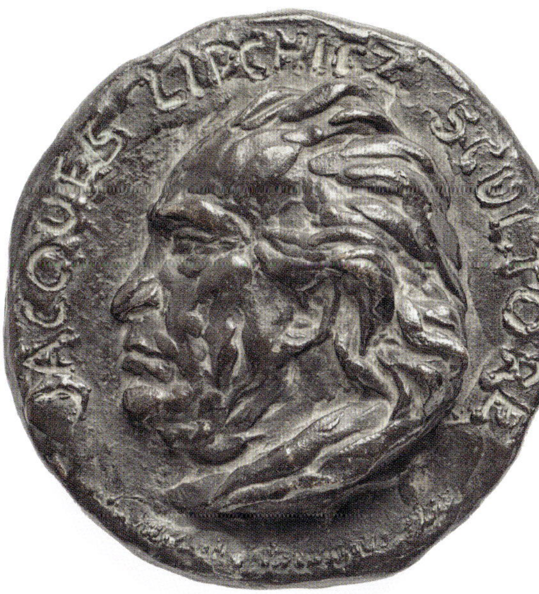
JACQUES LIPCHITZ SCULTORE

Cat. 20

[Cat. 21] page 108–109

BORIS TASLITZKY
(Paris, 1911 – Paris, 2005)
Portrait of Rubin Lipchitz, 1966
Pencil on paper, 697 × 694 mm
Signed u. r.: pour Jean [?] Boris Taslitzky 11.4.66
Private collection

Boris Taslitzky was born in Paris to parents who had fled to France at the time of the 1905 Russian Revolution. While he briefly participated in traditional academic training, he considered his master to be Jacques Lipchitz, whom he probably first met in the first half of the 1930s; he worked in Lipchitz's atelier until 1939. At the time, both were members of the Association des écrivains et artistes révolutionnaires (Association of Revolutionary Writers and Artists), made up of left-wing and communist intellectuals; they appeared together in the association's group exhibition in 1936. Encouraged by Lipchitz, Taslitzky regularly visited the collection of the Musée du Louvre, where he was greatly influenced by the works of, among others, Francisco de Goya (1746–1828), Eugène Delacroix, and — like his master — Théodore Géricault. A committed communist, Taslitzky became known as an exponent of French socialist realism in the 1930s with his monumental works recording contemporary events, but his portraiture is also significant. He remained in contact with the Lipchitz family even after the war, as is beautifully evidenced by his portrait of Jacques's younger brother, Rubin Lipchitz.

[DS]

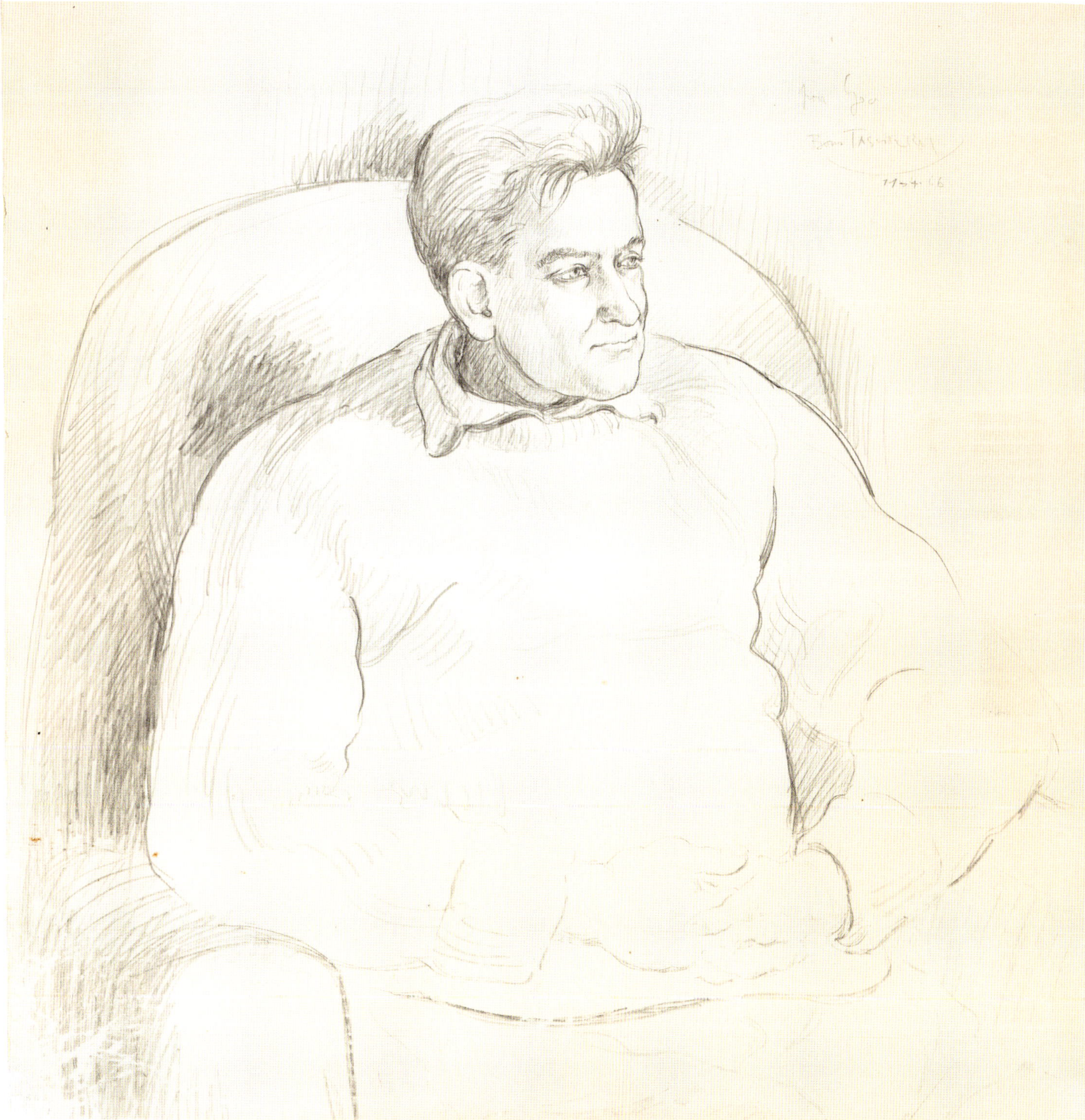

Cat. 21

BORIS TASLITZKY
(Paris, 1911 – Paris, 2005)
Portrait of a Young Man, 1959
Oil on canvas, 46 × 33 cm
Signed u. r.: Taslitzky 1959
Private collection

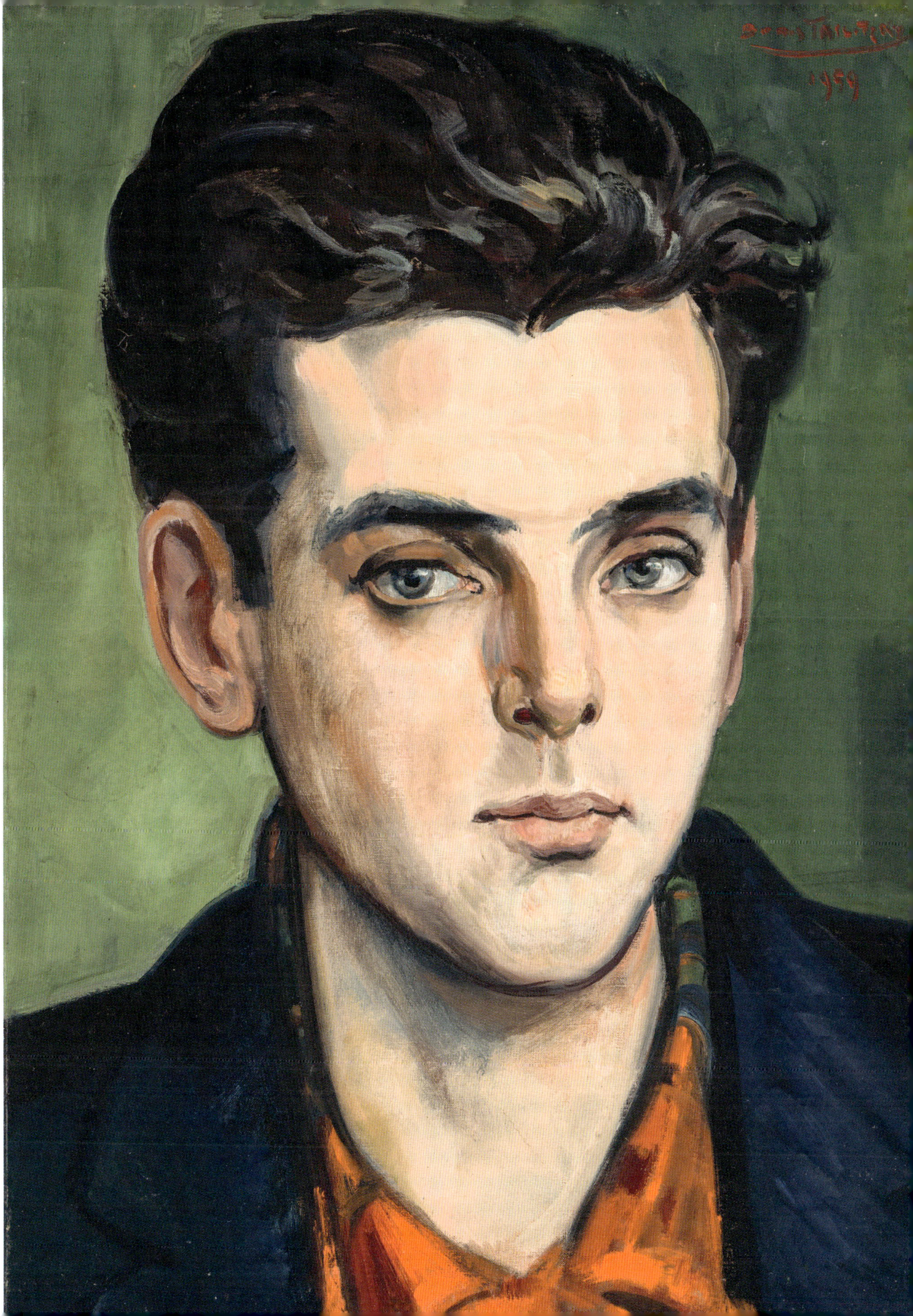
1959

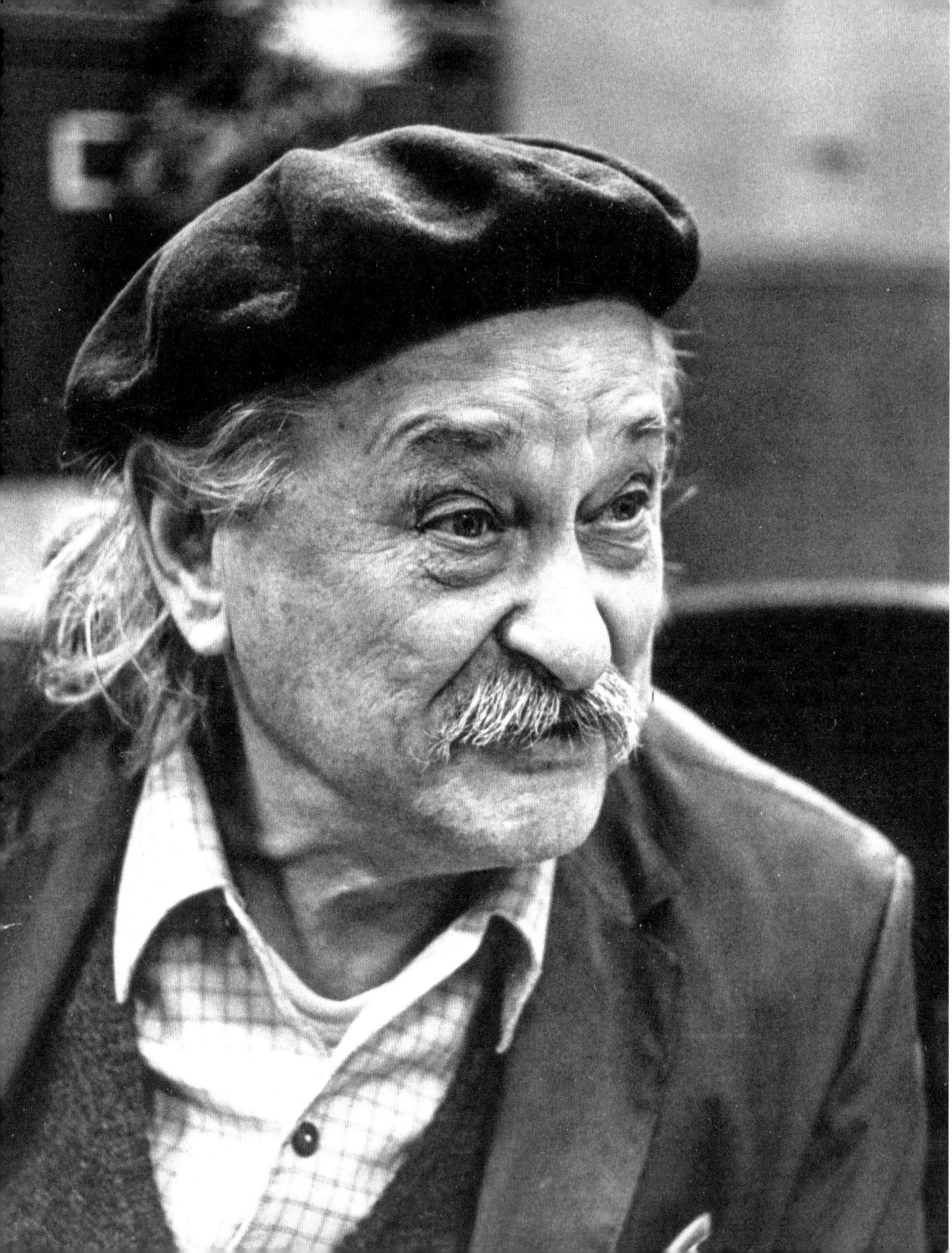

Compiled by Anett Somodi

BIOGRAPHICAL CHRONOLOGY

Jacques Lipchitz, ca. 1970
Private collection
‹

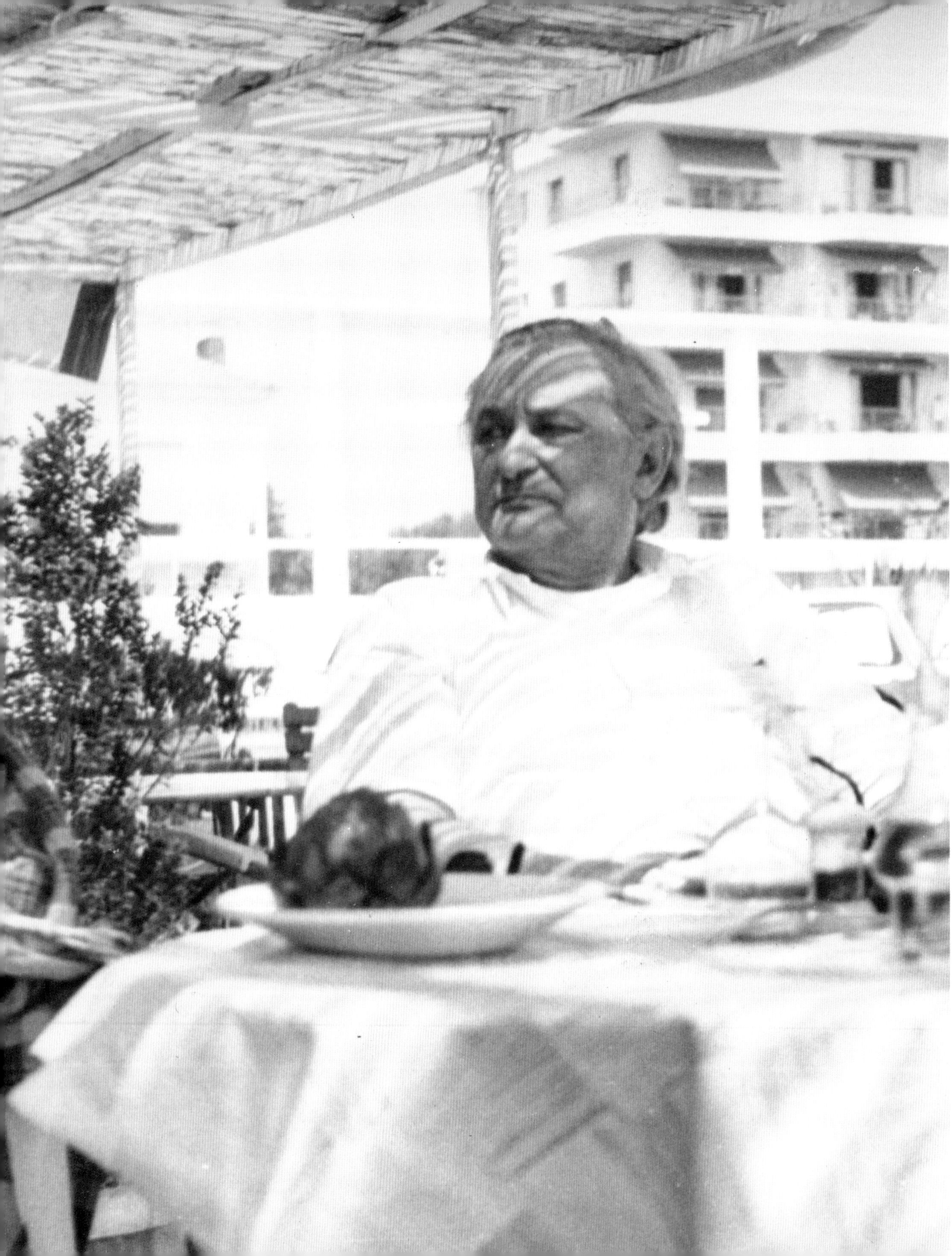

JACQUES LIPCHITZ (1891–1973)

22 August 1891

Chaim Jacob Lipchitz is born in Druskininkai (Russian Empire, now Lithuania). His mother was Rachel Leah Krinsky and his father was Abraham Lipchitz, a building contractor, and a member of a wealthy banking family.

1902–1906

He attends a commercial school in Białystok. Even in these years he spends much of his time drawing and making models in plaster.

1906–1909

He attends grammar school in Vilnius, graduating in 1909.

October 1909

Aged 18, he emigrates to Paris.

1909–1910

At the École des beaux-arts he is a pupil of Jean Antoine Injalbert, and he studies sculpture under Raoul Verlet at the Académie Julian. In the afternoons, he attends drawing classes at the Académie Colarossi. He regularly visits contemporary art galleries and the Musée du Louvre, where he takes special interest in ancient Greek, Roman, and Egyptian sculpture. He starts to collect tribal sculptures and artworks from different cultures.

1911–1912

He rents an atelier in Montparnasse. He makes the acquaintance of Diego Rivera and Max Jacob.

Jacques Lipchitz
in the South of France,
1960s
Private collection

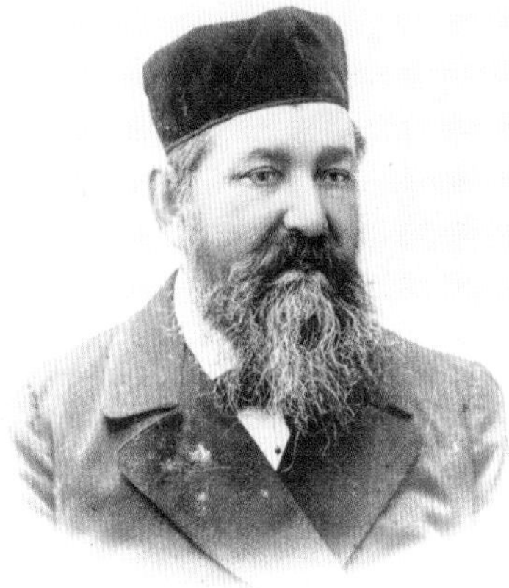

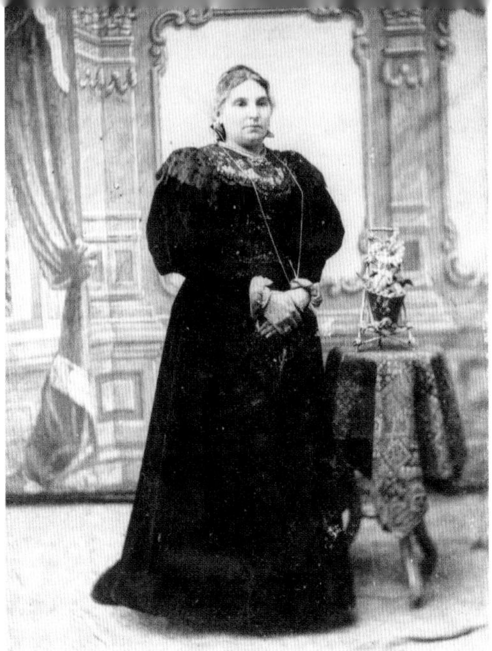

18 Jacques Lipchitz's paternal grandparents, David Issayev and Gima Lipchitz, Grodno
Private collection

1913

Through Diego Rivera he meets Pablo Picasso and other cubist artists, and becomes friends with Amedeo Modigliani (1884–1920). A few of his works are exhibited at the Salon d'Automne, and his *Woman and Gazelles* earns him the first prize for sculpture.

1914–1915

With Rivera and some other friends, he visits Mallorca and Spain. The outbreak of war forces them to stay on. In Barcelona he admires the buildings of Antoni Gaudí (1852–1926), and in Madrid he is enthralled by the paintings by El Greco (1541–1614), Diego Velázquez (1599–1660), and Jacopo Tintoretto (1518–1594) in the Prado. The journey enriches his art with new themes.

1915–1916

He meets the poet Berthe Kitrosser, who later becomes his wife. Their marriage is immortalised in a double portrait by Amadeo Modigliani (see page 6). Lipchitz produces his first mature cubist sculptures.

1916

He meets Juan Gris, and they become close friends and colleagues. Lipchitz signs a contract with the art dealer Léonce Rosenberg, a supporter of numerous cubist artists, including the painter André Lhote.

1918

In spring, when Paris is threatened by German bombing, he leaves the city with his wife and Juan Gris. As sculptural materials are unavailable, he makes drawings and

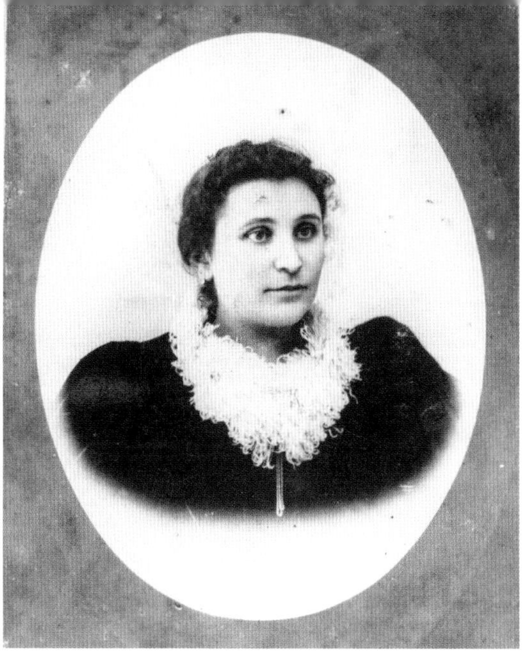
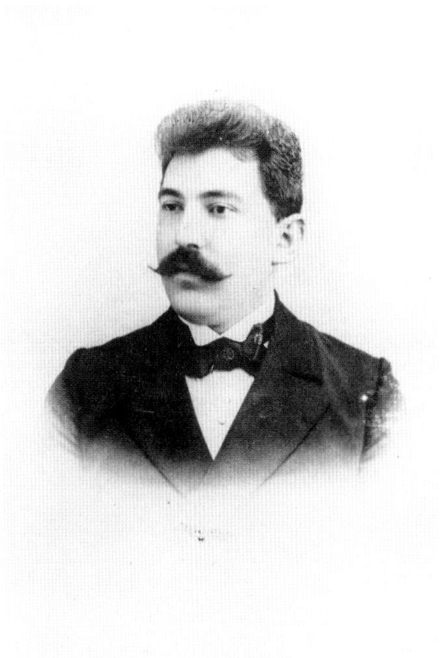

19 Jacques Lipchitz's parents, Rachel Leah Krinsky and Abraham Lipchitz, Grodno Private collection

sketches. He is in contact with Modigliani, Max Jacob, Jean Cocteau (1889–1963), and the writer Raymond Radiguet (1903–1923).

1920
Léonce Rosenberg organises Lipchitz's first solo exhibition in the Galerie L'Effort Moderne, and then they terminate their contract. The first monograph on Lipchitz's work is published, written by Maurice Raynal (1884–1954).

1922
He meets the American art collector Dr Albert C. Barnes, who purchases eight sculptures from him and provides him with further commissions.

1925
He moves to Boulogne-sur-Seine, a suburb of Paris, to a house and studio designed by Le Corbusier. His sculpture takes a new direction with his "transparent" series. His bronze sculptures are made with the lost-wax process.

1926
Jacques's seventeen-year-old brother, Rubin, moves to his home in Paris; years later, as an engineer, he will manage the artist's affairs and exhibitions in Europe.

1927–1928
He is deeply shocked by the deaths, in quick succession, of Juan Gris, his own father, and one of his younger sisters.

1930

At his first major retrospective, a hundred of his works are exhibited in Paris's Galerie de la Renaissance. He creates his first works on mythological and biblical themes, foremost of which is *Prometheus*.

1934

His mother dies.

1935

His first major exhibition in the USA is held at the Brummer Gallery, New York.

1936–1937

Commissioned by the French government, he creates the large plaster sculpture *Prometheus and the Vulture* for the entrance to the Science Pavilion at the Exposition Internationale in Paris. Picasso's *Guernica* is exhibited in the Spanish Pavilion. At the end of the World's Fair, the plaster sculpture is demolished.

Until 1939

The young painter Boris Taslitzky, whom Lipchitz met in the 1930s, works in the master's studio in Boulogne-sur-Seine.

1940

He flees to Toulouse to escape the invading German army; he decides to emigrate.

13 June 1941

He arrives in New York.

1942

He exhibits regularly in New York's Buchholz Gallery (later Curt Valentin Gallery); he casts his sculptures in the city's Modern Art Foundry. His works become increasingly monumental.

1946

He exhibits at the Galerie Maeght in Paris, travelling to the event with his wife. Berthe decides to stay in Paris, and they divorce. He is awarded the Légion d'Honneur. On his return to the United States, he settles in Hastings-on-Hudson.

1948

He marries the sculptor Yulla Halberstadt, with whom he has a daughter, Lolya Rachel.

5 January 1952
Fire in his New York studio destroys much of his work as well as a substantial part of his valuable art collection. He works temporarily in the Modern Art Foundry, until his new studio is built in Hastings-on-Hudson.

1954
A retrospective of his work opens at The Museum of Modern Art (MoMA), New York; in the following years, shows are held around Europe (Amsterdam, Otterlo, Basel, Dortmund, Paris, Brussels, London).

1960s
He produces the first models for the work entitled *Our Tree of Life*, commissioned by the Hadassah University Hospital of Jerusalem.

1961–1962
He begins his collaboration with New York's Otto Gerson Gallery (now Marlborough Gallery). He discovers Italy, and from now on he spends every summer in Pietrasanta, where he works on his monumental sculptures in the foundry of Luigi Tommasi.

1964
His work entitled *Between Heaven and Earth* is included in the *documenta III International Exhibition* in Kassel.

1972
His biography, *My Life in Sculpture*, is published to coincide with a major exhibition of his work at The Metropolitan Museum of Art, New York.

26 May 1973
Jacques Lipchitz dies on the island of Capri; he is buried in Jerusalem.

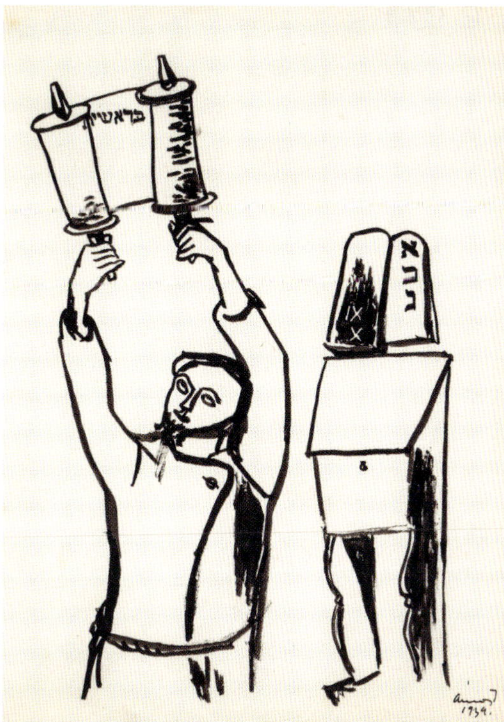

20 Imre Ámos, *The Feast of the Giving of the Torah*, 1940
Museum of Fine Arts, Budapest
(XXth-Century Foundation)

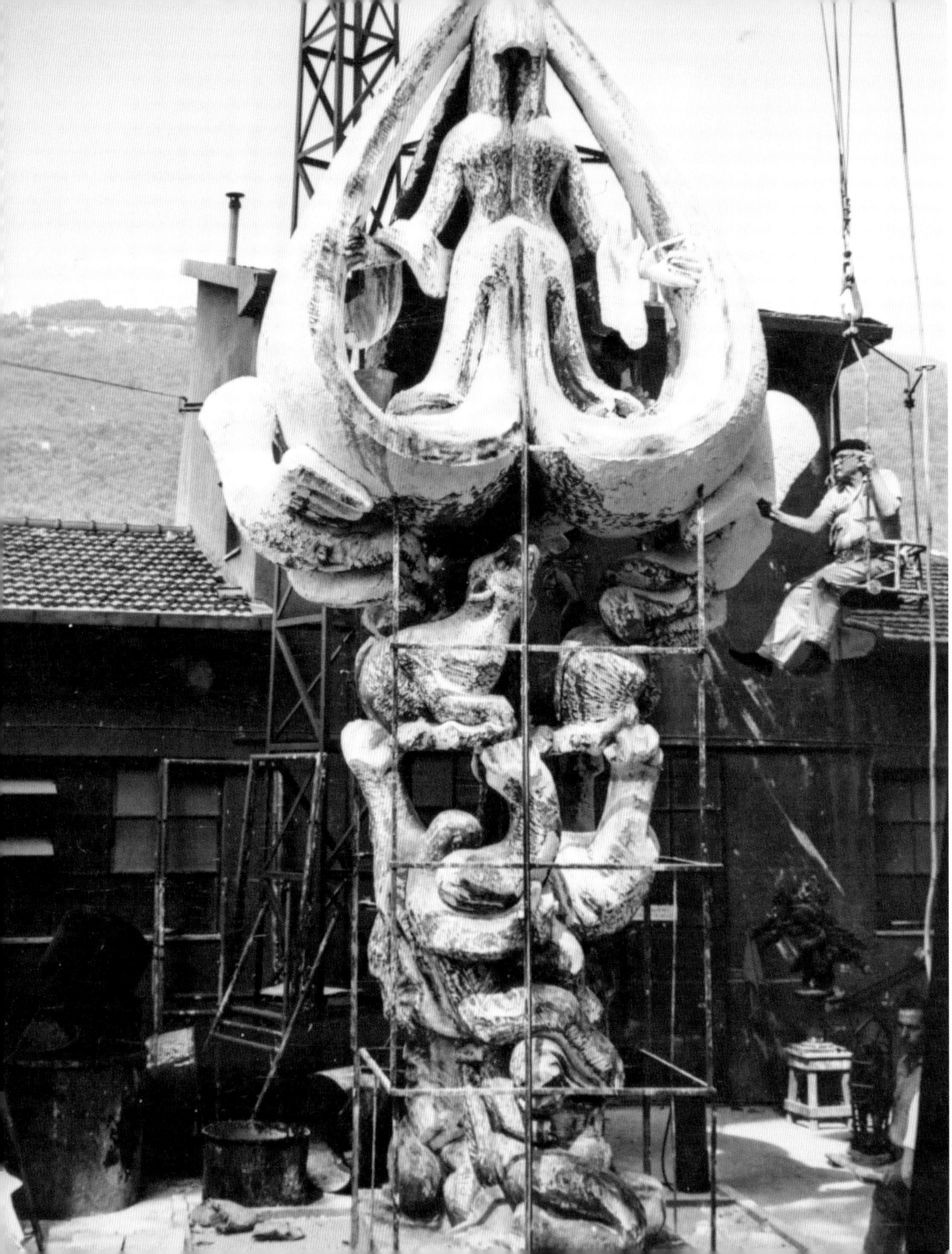

Compiled by Dominika Sodics

SELECTED BIBLIOGRAPHY

Jacques Lipchitz working
on his sculpture *Peace on Earth* (1967–1969),
Fonderia Luigi Tommasi, Pietrasanta, Italy
Private collection

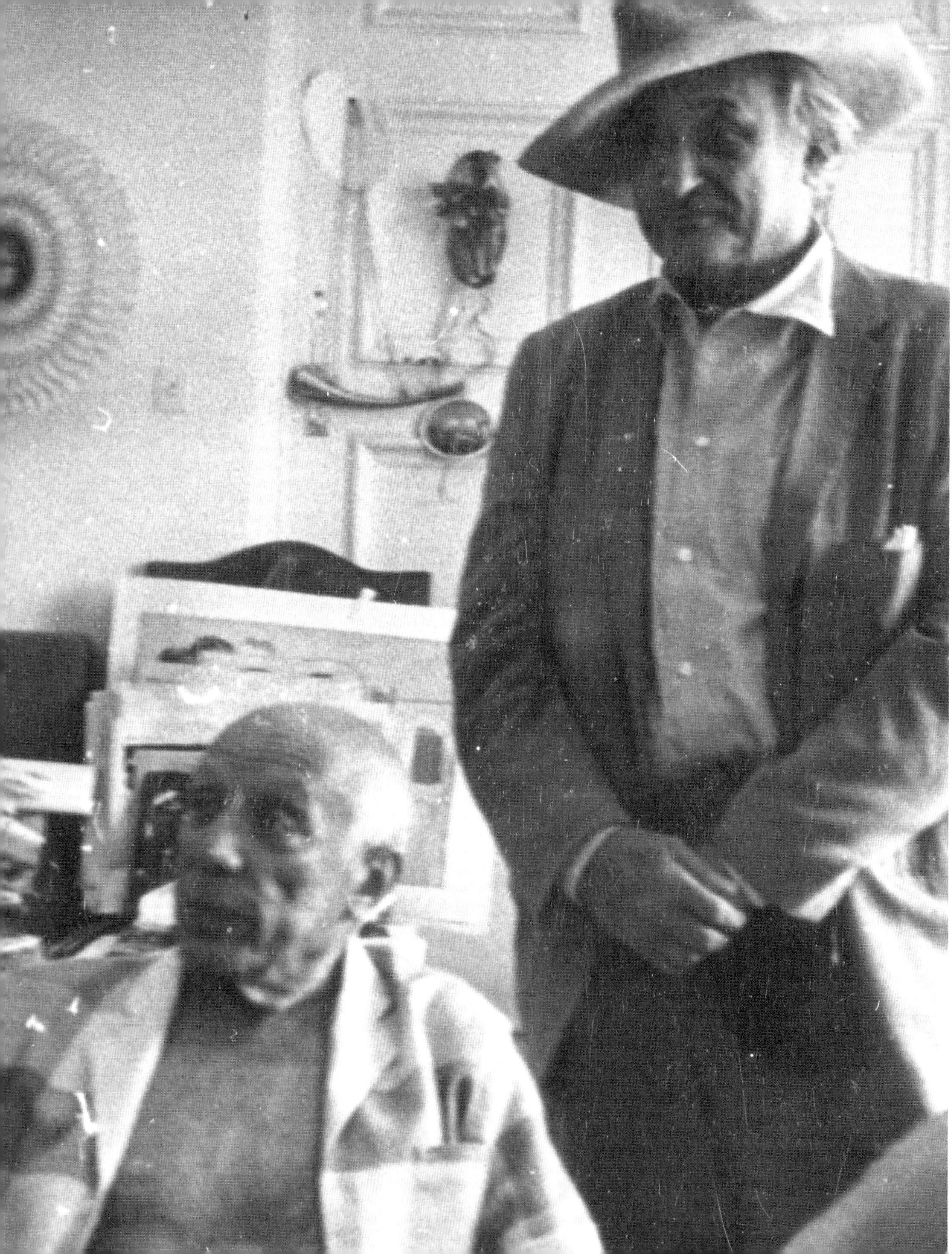

1920
Dermée, Paul. "Lipchitz." *L'Esprit nouveau* (Paris), no. 2 (1920): 169–83.
Raynal, Maurice. *Lipchitz*. Paris: Action, 1920.
1926
Waldemar-George. "Bronzes de Jacques Lipchitz." *L'Amour de l'art*, September 1926, 299–302.
1929
Vitrac, Roger. *Jacques Lipchitz*. Collections les sculpteurs français nouveaux 7. Paris: NRF, Gallimard, 1929.
1935
Faure, Élie. *Jacques Lipchitz*. Translated by Allan Ross MacDougall. Exhibition catalogue. New York: Brummer Gallery, 1935.
1947
Raynal, Maurice. *Jacques Lipchitz*. Paris: Jeanne Bucher, 1947.
1950
Faure, Élie. "Jacques Lipchitz et le cubisme." *Arts Plastiques* (Brussels), no. 2 (1950): 117–22.
1954
Hope, Henry R. *The Sculpture of Jacques Lipchitz*. Exhibition catalogue. New York: Museum of Modern Art, 1954.
1961
Patai, Irene. *Encounters. The Life of Jacques Lipchitz.* New York: Funk & Wagnalls, 1961.
1963
Lipchitz, Jacques. *157 Small Bronze Sketches 1914–1962*. Exhibition catalogue. New York: Otto Gerson Gallery, 1963.
1969
Arnason, H. Harvard. *Jacques Lipchitz. Sketches in Bronze*. New York: Praeger; London: Pall Mall, 1969.

Jacques Lipchitz and Pablo Picasso in the South of France, ca. 1968
Private collection
‹

1971
Weyl, Martin, and Willem Sandberg. *Jacques Lipchitz. Bronze Sketches. The Reuven Lipchitz Collection*. Exhibition catalogue. Jerusalem: Israel Museum, 1971.
1972
Lipchitz, Jacques, and H. Harvard Arnason. *My Life in Sculpture.* New York: The Viking Press, 1972.
1975
Hammacher, Abraham M. *Jacques Lipchitz*. Translated by James Brockway. New York: Harry N. Abrams, 1975.
1978
Stott, Deborah A. *Jacques Lipchitz and Cubism*. New York — London: Garland, 1978.
1986
Jenkins, David Fraser, and Derek Pullen. *The Lipchitz Gift. Models for Sculptures.* Exhibition catalogue. London: Tate Gallery, 1986.
1989
Wilkinson, Alan G. *Jacques Lipchitz. A Life in Sculpture*. Exhibition catalogue. Toronto: Art Gallery of Ontario, 1989.
1991
Yifat, Dorit. *Jacques Lipchitz. From Sketch to Sculpture*. Exhibition catalogue. Tel Aviv: Tel Aviv Museum of Art, 1991.
1996
Wilkinson, Alan G. *The Sculpture of Jacques Lipchitz. A Catalogue Raisonné. The Paris Years, 1910–1940*. Volume 1. London: Thames & Hudson, 1996.
1997
Lipchitz. Un mundo sorprendido en el espacio. Exhibition catalogue. Madrid: Museo Nacional Centro de Arte Reina Sofía; Valencia: IVAM, Centre Julio González, 1997.
Letters to Lipchitz, and Some Personal Notes by the Artist. Edited by J. F. Yvars and Lucía Ybarra. Madrid: Museo Nacional Centro de Arte Reina Sofia, 1997.
2000
Wilkinson, Alan G. *The Sculpture of Jacques Lipchitz, A Catalogue Raisonné. The American Years, 1941–1973*. Volume 2. New York: Thames & Hudson, 2000.
2001
Lipchitz and the Avant-Garde. From Paris to New York. Exhibition catalogue. Edited by Josef Helfenstein and Jordana Mendelson. Campaign: University of Illinois Urbana-Champaign, 2001.
2002
Pütz, Catherine. *Jacques Lipchitz. The First Cubist Sculptor.* London: Paul Holberton Publishing in association with Lund Humphries, 2002.

2004
Jacques Lipchitz. Collections du Centre Pompidou, Musée national d'art moderne et du Musée des beaux-arts de Nancy. Exhibition catalogue. Musée des beaux-arts, Nancy — Musée des beaux-arts et de la dentelle, Calais. Edited by Brigitte Leal. Paris: Centre Pompidou, 2004.
2005
Lipchitz. Les années françaises de 1910 à 1940. Exhibition catalogue. Musée des Années 1930 de Boulogne-Billancourt. Somogy éditions d'art — Association des Amis du musée des Années 30, Boulogne-Billancourt. Paris, 2005.
2009
Barañano, Kosme María de. *Jacques Lipchitz. The Plasters. A Catalogue Raisonné 1911–1973*. Bilbao: Bilbao Bizkaia Kutxa Fundazioak, 2009.
Pütz, Catherine. *Jacques Lipchitz. Master Drawings. The Anatomy of a Sculptor.* Exhibition catalogue. London: Ben Uri Gallery, 2009.
2017
The Lipchitz Collection in the Israel Museum, Jerusalem. Exhibition catalogue. Edited by Tanya Sirakovich. Jerusalem: Israel Museum, 2017.
Jacques Lipchitz. Bildhauer des 20. Jahrhunderts. Edited by Ingrid Mössinger, Karin Sagner, and Diana Kopka. Exhibition catalogue. Chemnitz: Kunstsammlungen Chemnitz; Dresden: Sandstein, 2017.
2018
Jacques Lipchitz (1891–1973). A Retrospective. Exhibition catalogue. Moscow: Museum of Modern Art, 2018.
2019
Barañano, Kosme María de. *Jacques Lipchitz. The Paris Years. Sculpture and Drawings 1911–1932*. Exhibition catalogue. New York: Marlborough Gallery, 2019.

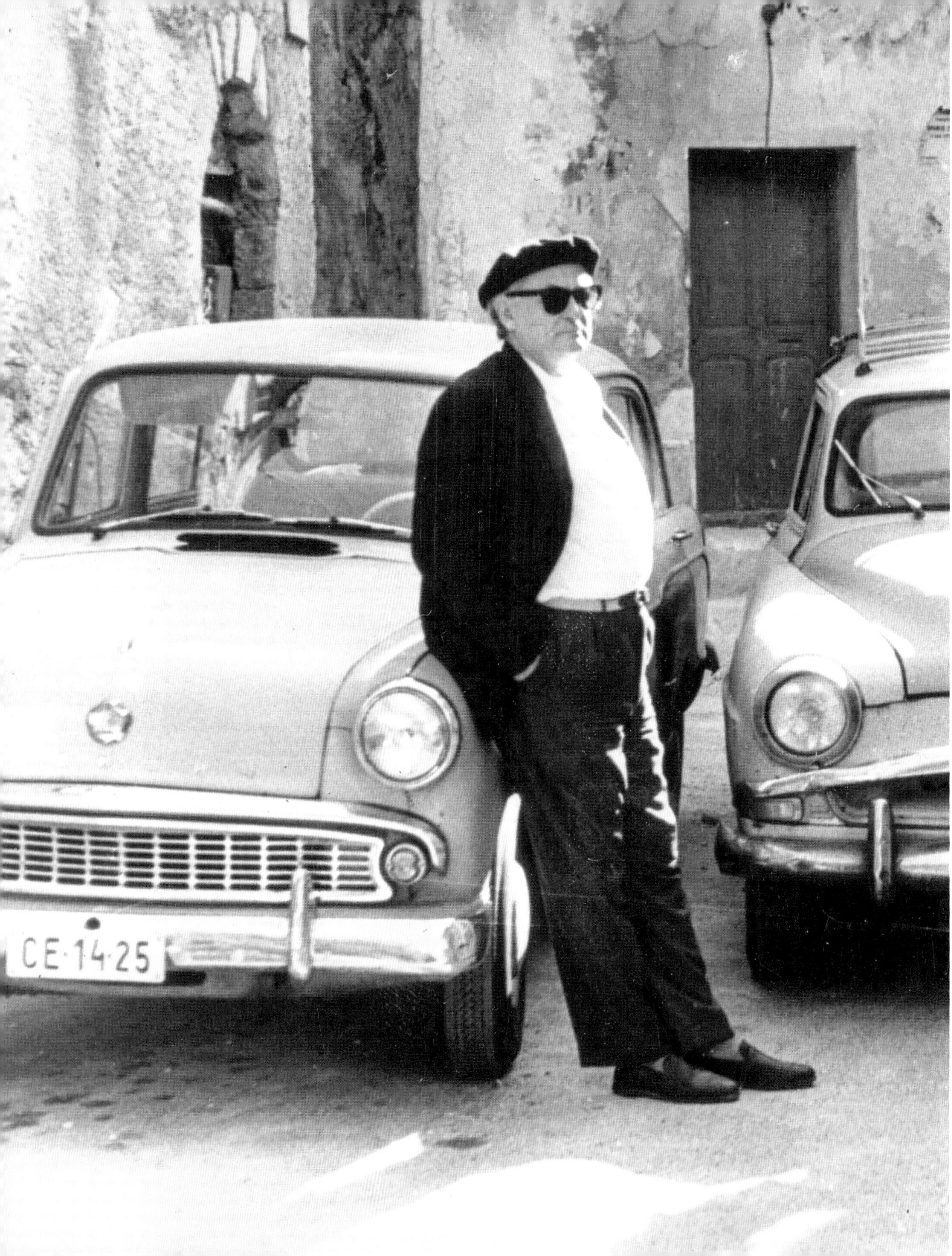
CE·14·25

APPENDIX

Jacques Lipchitz
in the South of France, ca. 1968
Private collection

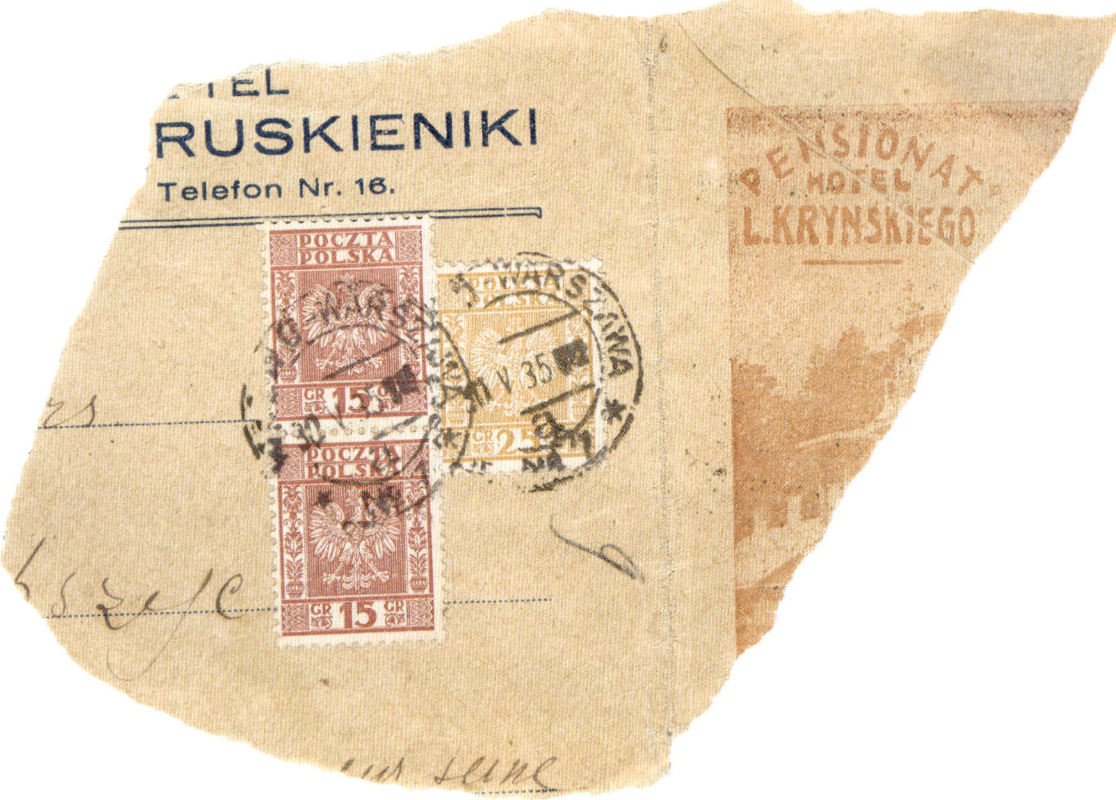
TEL
RUSKIENIKI
Telefon Nr. 16.
POCZTA POLSKA
15 GR
PENSJONAT
HOTEL
L. KRYNSKIEGO

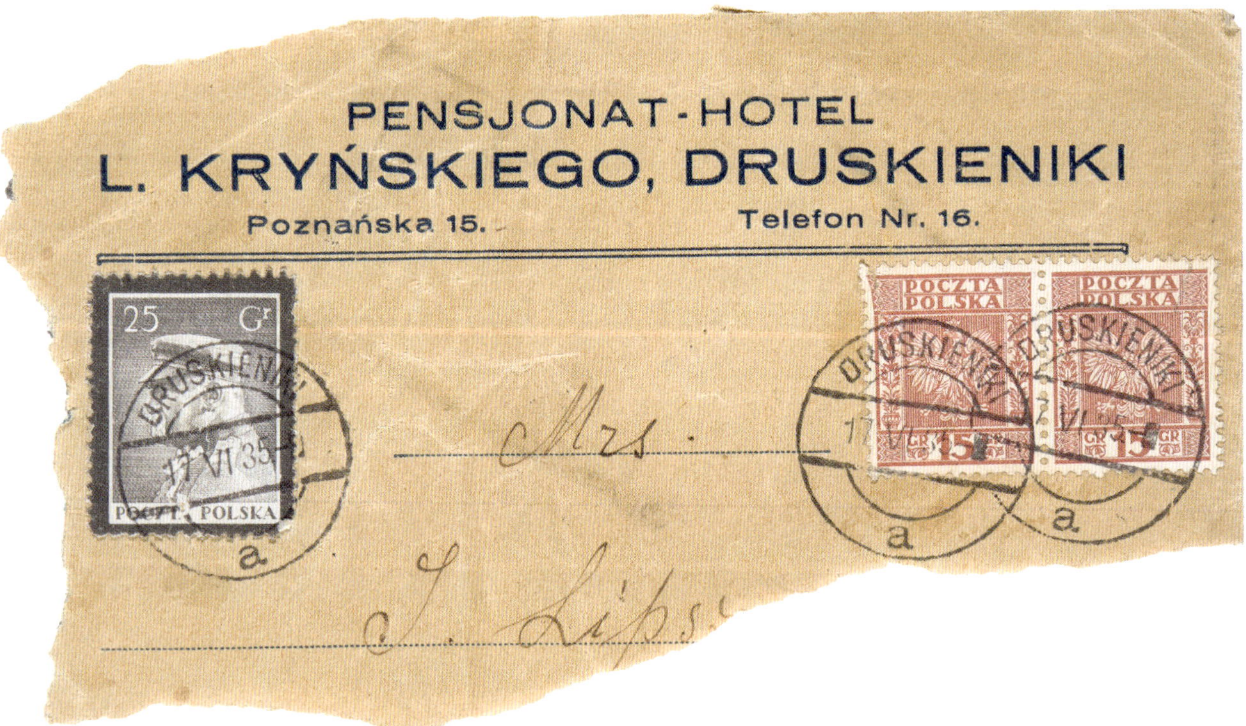
PENSJONAT-HOTEL
L. KRYŃSKIEGO, DRUSKIENIKI
Poznańska 15.
Telefon Nr. 16.
25 Gr
POCZTA POLSKA
DRUSKIENIKI
17 VI 35
Mrs

LIST OF EXHIBITED WORKS

Cat. 1
JACQUES LIPCHITZ
(Druskininkai, 1891 – Capri, 1973)
Seated Pierrot, 1922
Lead, 34 × 14.2 × 13.5 cm
Signed: J.L. 3/7., 22.
Private collection
Wilkinson cat. 136

Cat. 2
JACQUES LIPCHITZ
(Druskininkai, 1891 – Capri, 1973)
Woman with a Guitar, 1923–1924
Bronze, 15.7 × 23.1 × 3.8 cm
Signed: J.L. 6/7; foundry stamp: Georges Rudier. Fondeur. Paris.
Private collection
Wilkinson cat. 150

Cat. 3
JACQUES LIPCHITZ
(Druskininkai, 1891 – Capri, 1973)
Sculpture Design (Figure with a Guitar), early 1920s (?)
Pen and ink on paper, 193 × 80 mm
Private collection

Cat. 4
ANDRÉ LHOTE
(Bordeaux, 1885 – Paris, 1962)
Night Party in Montparnasse, at the Bal Bullier, 1922
Colour lithograph on paper, 1380 × 990 mm
Private collection

Cat. 5
JACQUES LIPCHITZ
(Druskininkai, 1891 – Capri, 1973)
Towards a New World, maquette no. 4, 1934
Bronze, 19.3 × 19.2 × 8 cm
Signed: Lipchitz 5/7
Private collection
Wilkinson cat. 321

Cat. 6
JACQUES LIPCHITZ
(Druskininkai, 1891 – Capri, 1973)
Prometheus and the Vulture. Pages from the portfolio: Jacques Lipchitz, *12 dessins pour Prométhée* (Paris: Jeanne Bucher, 1940)
Collotype prints with pochoir on paper, approximately 420 × 310 mm
Private collection

Cat. 7
JACQUES LIPCHITZ
(Druskininkai, 1891 – Capri, 1973)
Theseus and the Minotaur, 1943
Aquatint on paper, 566 × 380 mm
Signed l. r.: Lipchitz; l. l.: 28/50
Private collection

Cat. 8
JACQUES LIPCHITZ
(Druskininkai, 1891 – Capri, 1973)
The Road to Exile, 1944
Etching and aquatint on paper, 513 × 331 mm
Signed l. r.: Lipchitz; l. l.: 32/33
Private collection

Fragments of letters from Jacques Lipchitz to his wife
Warsaw, 30 May 1935;
Druskieniki [Druskininkai], 17 June 1935
Private collection

Cat. 9
JACQUES LIPCHITZ
(Druskininkai, 1891 – Capri, 1973)
Pages from the portfolio: *The Drawings of Jacques Lipchitz* (New York: Curt Valentin, 1944)
Collotype prints, 380 × 280 mm
Private collection

Cat. 10
JACQUES LIPCHITZ
(Druskininkai, 1891 – Capri, 1973)
Nude and Cock, 1945
Aquatint and drypoint on paper, 306 × 230 mm
Signed l. r.: Lipchitz; l. l.: 10/50
Private collection

Cat. 11
AMÉDÉE OZENFANT
(Saint-Quentin, 1886 – Cannes, 1966)
Harmonics, ca. 1960
Lithograph on paper, 1044 × 744 mm
Signed l. r.: Ozenfant 41/110
Private collection

Cat. 12
AMÉDÉE OZENFANT
(Saint-Quentin, 1886 – Cannes, 1966)
Maternity II (Entwined Silhouettes), 1960
Lithograph on paper, 635 × 495 mm
Signed l. r.: Ozenfant 70/115
Museum of Fine Arts, Budapest, inv. no. L.85.48

Cat. 13
JACQUES LIPCHITZ
(Druskininkai, 1891 – Capri, 1973)
Sketch for *Our Tree of Life*, version II, 1971–1972
Bronze, 23 × 15 × 8.5 cm
Cast: Fonderia Luigi Tommasi, Pietrasanta
Signed: Lipchitz 4/7
Private collection
Wilkinson cat. 739

Cat. 14
JACQUES LIPCHITZ
(Druskininkai, 1891 – Capri, 1973)
Sketch for *Our Tree of Life*, version IV, 1971–1972
Bronze, 47 × 15.5 × 11.5 cm
Signed: Lipchitz 6/7
Private collection
Wilkinson cat. 741

Cat. 15
ARBIT BLATAS
(Kaunas, 1908 – New York, 1999)
Portrait of Jacques Lipchitz, 1962
Lithograph on paper, 498 × 326 mm
Private collection

Cat. 16
JACQUES LIPCHITZ
(Druskininkai, 1891 – Capri, 1973)
Small study for *The Rape of Europa*, 1969–1970
Bronze, 13 × 11.2 × 7.5 cm
Private collection
Wilkinson cat. 681

Cat. 17
JACQUES LIPCHITZ
(Druskininkai, 1891 – Capri, 1973)
The Rape of Europa, ca. 1970
Crayon on paper, 320 × 236 mm
Private collection

Cats. 18 and 19
JACQUES LIPCHITZ
(Druskininkai, 1891 – Capri, 1973)
Medallion with Self-Portrait (recto and verso), 1967
Bronze, diameter: 11 cm

Inscription: JACQUES LIPCHITZ SCULTORE 1967
Private collection

Cat. 20
BORIS TASLITZKY
(Paris, 1911 – Paris, 2005)
Portrait of Rubin Lipchitz, 1966
Pencil on paper, 697 × 694 mm
Signed u. r.: pour Jean [?] Boris Taslitzky 11.4.66
Private collection

Cat. 21
BORIS TASLITZKY
(Paris, 1911 – Paris, 2005)
Portrait of a Young Man, 1959
Oil on canvas, 46 × 33 cm
Signed u. r.: Taslitzky 1959
Private collection

LIST OF ILLUSTRATIONS

ESSAYS

Page 6
Amedeo Modigliani
Jacques and Berthe Lipchitz, 1916
Oil on canvas, 81.3 × 54.3 cm
The Art Institute of Chicago, Chicago,
inv. no. 1926.221
Helen Birch Bartlett Memorial Collection
Photo © The Art Institute of Chicago

Page 8
Jacques and Rubin Lipchitz with company in front of the Chapel of the Rosary in Vence, ca. 1968
Photo
Private collection
Photo © Museum of Fine Arts, Budapest

1 Druskieniki, early 20th century
Archive postcard
Published by A. G. Syrkin
Photo © www.miestai.net

2 Panorama of Vilna (Vilnius), ca. 1910
Archive postcard
Photo © Alamy Stock Photo

3 View of the Eiffel Tower, Paris, 1910
Photo © Pictures Now / Alamy Stock Photo

4 George Moffett
Jacques Lipchitz's studio
at Hastings-on-Hudson, USA, ca. 1950
Photo, silver bromide gelatine print, 21 × 26 cm
Musée d'art et d'histoire du Judaïsme, Paris,
inv. no. PH/Fds Lipchitz PE 36.1
Donation of Rubin Lipchitz
Photo © mahJ, Musée d'art et d'histoire
du Judaïsme

5a Jacques Lipchitz
Géricault, 1933
Terracotta, 24.1 × 17.7 × 20.2 cm
Donation of the Lipchitz Foundation, 1982
The Tate Gallery, London, inv. no. To3494
© The Estate of Jacques Lipchitz courtesy,
Marlborough Gallery, New York

5b Jacques Lipchitz
Géricault, maquette no. 2, 1933
Bronze, 7 copies, 17.5 cm
The Israel Museum, Jerusalem, inv. no. B70.0812
Gift of Rubin Lipchitz, Paris, in memory
of Abraham and Rachel Lea Lipchitz
Photo © The Israel Museum, Jerusalem

6 Boris Taslitzky
Hommage to Théodore Géricault and Jacques Lipchitz, 1937
Oil on canvas, 50 × 75.2 cm

Musée des beaux-arts de Rouen, Rouen,
inv. no. 2004.6.1
© C. Lancien, C. Loisel / Réunion des Musées Métropolitains Rouen Normandie

7 Jacques Lipchitz and Pablo Picasso in the South of France, ca. 1968
Photo
Private collection
Photo © Museum of Fine Arts, Budapest

8 Henry Moore
Sculpture Designs, 1949
Lithograph on paper, 497 × 765 mm
Museum of Fine Arts, Budapest,
inv. no. L.87.10
© The Henry Moore Foundation. All Rights Reserved, DACS / HUNGART 2024
Photo © Museum of Fine Arts, Budapest

9 Eduardo Chillida
Lurra G-124, 1989
Fire chamotte clay, glaze, 15.5 × 21 × 21 cm
Museum of Fine Arts, Budapest,
inv. no. 2014.3.U
© Zabalaga Leku, HUNGART, Budapest 2024
Photo © Museum of Fine Arts, Budapest

10 Books on Théodore Géricault in the library of Jacques Lipchitz
Photo © Museum of Fine Arts, Budapest

11 Jerusalem Old City, an aerial view of Temple Mount, 1995
Photo © Hanan Isachar / Alamy Stock Photo

Page 23
Marc Vaux, The wooden structure of Lipchitz's sculpture *Prometheus and the Vulture* (1937) in the artist's studio in Boulogne-sur-Seine
Photo
Private collection
Photo © Museum of Fine Arts, Budapest

12 Statuette of Nereid Riding a Sea Monster
Egypt, Coptic (?), 4th–5th centuries
Bronze, 5.5 × 20 × 5 mm
The Israel Museum, Jerusalem,
inv. no. B06.0548
© The Israel Museum, Jerusalem by Elie Posner

13 "Cabinet of Curiosities", on display at the Jacques Lipchitz Collection
Curator: Tanya Sirakovich
Design: Studio de Lange
The Israel Museum, Jerusalem
Gift of the Lipchitz Family
© The Israel Museum, Jerusalem by Elie Posner, 2010

14 Jacques Lipchitz
Final sketch for *Our Tree of Life*, 1973
Plaster, 147 × 76 × 86 cm
The Israel Museum, Jerusalem,
inv. no. B03.1132
Gift of the Jacques and Yulla Lipchitz Foundation, Inc. (gift of the Lipchitz Family to the American Friends of The Israel Museum)
© Estate of Jacques Lipchitz / The Israel Museum, Jerusalem by Elie Posner

15 Jacques Lipchitz
The Struggle, 1973
Plaster, diameter: 45.5 cm
The Israel Museum, Jerusalem,
inv. no. B75.0716
© Estate of Jacques Lipchitz /
Photo © The Israel Museum, Jerusalem

CATALOGUE

16 Jacques Lipchitz
Reclining Nude with Guitar, 1928
Marble, 41.6 × 70.3 × 34.3 cm
The Museum of Modern Art, New York,
inv. no. 182.1994
Blanchette Hooker Rockefeller Bequest

17 Arbit Blatas
Statue of Jacques Lipchitz, 1991
Garden of Boulogne-Billancourt Town Hall
Photo
Private collection
Photo © Museum of Fine Arts, Budapest

Page 110
Jacques Lipchitz, ca. 1970
Photo
Private collection
Photo © Museum of Fine Arts, Budapest

Page 112
Jacques Lipchitz in the South of France, 1960s
Photo
Private collection
Photo © Museum of Fine Arts, Budapest

CHRONOLOGY

18 Jacques Lipchitz's paternal grandparents,
David Issayev and Gima Lipchitz
Photo, Grodno
Private collection
Photo © Museum of Fine Arts, Budapest

19 Jacques Lipchitz's parents, Rachel Leah
Krinsky and Abraham Lipchitz
Photo, Grodno
Private collection
Photo © Museum of Fine Arts, Budapest

20 Imre Ámos
The Feast of the Giving of the Torah, 1940
India ink on paper, 295 × 225 mm
Museum of Fine Arts, Budapest
(XXth-Century Foundation)

Page 118
Jacques Lipchitz working
on his sculpture *Peace on Earth*
(1967–1969), Fonderia Luigi Tommasi,
Pietrasanta, Italy
Photo
Private collection
Photo © Museum of Fine Arts, Budapest

Page 120
Jacques Lipchitz and Pablo Picasso
in the South of France, ca. 1968
Photo
Private collection
Photo © Museum of Fine Arts, Budapest

Page 124
Jacques Lipchitz in the South of France,
ca. 1968
Photo
Private collection
Photo © Museum of Fine Arts, Budapest

Page 126
Fragments of letters from
Jacques Lipchitz to his wife
Warsaw, 30 May 1935;
Druskieniki [Druskininkai], 17 June, 1935
Private collection
Photo © Museum of Fine Arts, Budapest

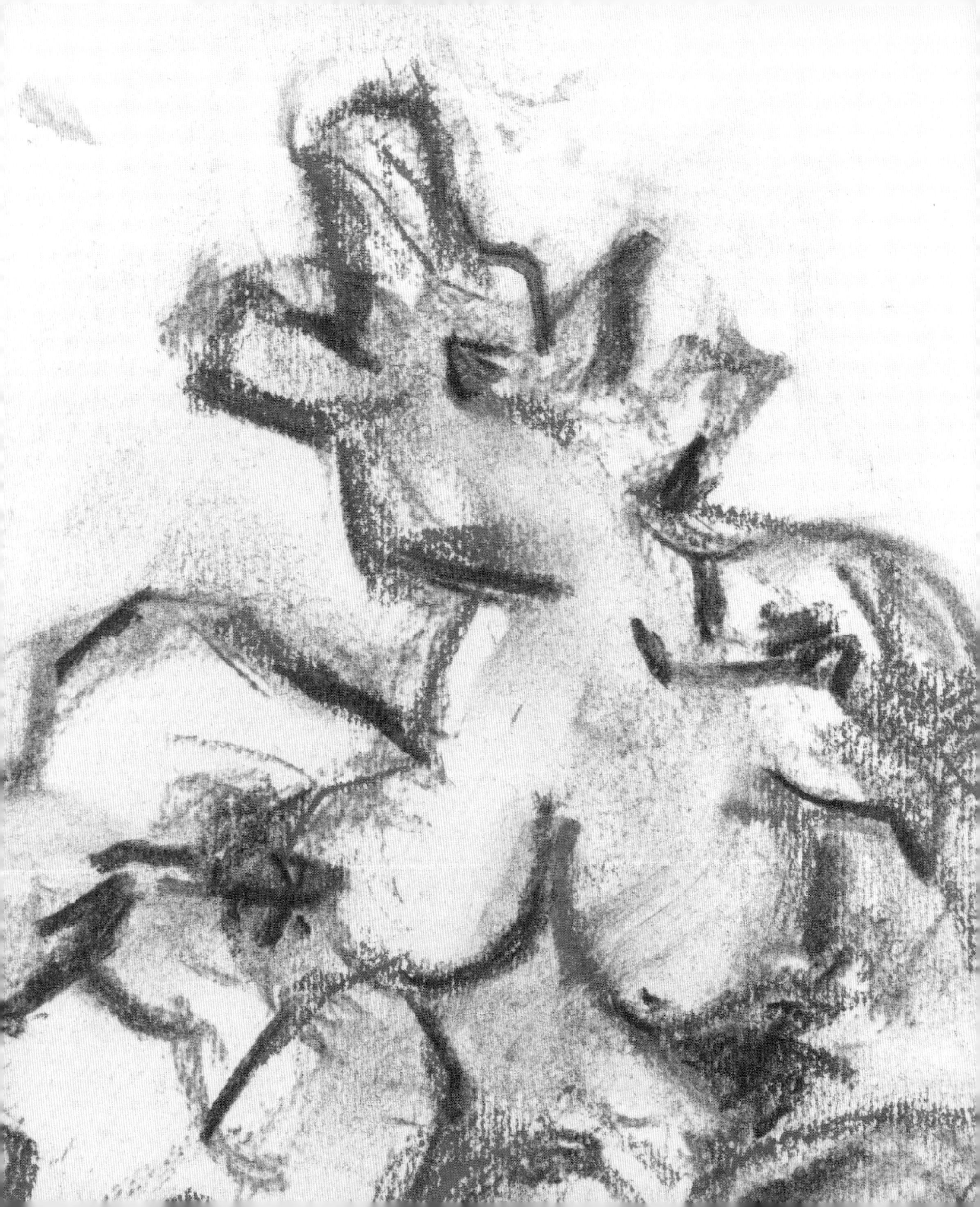

Cat. 17
Jacques Lipchitz
The Rape of Europa, ca. 1970
Private collection

EXHIBITION

Concept of the exhibition: Judit GESKÓ and Anett SOMODI
Assistant to the curators: Dominika SODICS
Exhibition management: Krisztina SZVOBODA

Registrar: Zsófia FARKAS
Legal tasks: Henriett GALAMBOS, Adrienn GIPPERT
Financial tasks: Enikő CSER, Szilvia ZALKA
Installation design: Zsuzsanna BROTESSER
Lighting: UNISOL Installációs Kft. Gábor BAKTAI

Exhibition texts:
Judit GESKÓ, Kata BODOR, Márton OROSZ, Dominika SODICS, Anett SOMODI
Translation: Steve KANE
Copy editors: Noémi BÖRÖCZKI, Helga RUTTKAY
Museum education: Szilvia ZÁRAY
Conservators: Eszter BAKONYI, Ágota KOVÁCSNÉ GŐGÖS, Erzsébet MÓZER, Borbála ORSZÁGH, István PANKASZI
Communication and marketing: Tibor BARCSIK, Barbara BERGENDY, Júlia GOTTFRIED, Laura KUND, Zsófi LÁSZLÓ, Zoltán LÉVAY, Boróka PÉNZES, Dávid SZABÓ, Anna VIDÁK-SARKANTYU
Communication design: Zsuzsanna BROTESSER
Reproduction rights of the exhibition hall: Szilvia CSEH
Sponsorship manager: Lili HORVÁTH, Balázs KÉGLI
Art handlers: Installation technicians of the museum
Visitor services: Anna DARÓCZI, Ágota NAGY, Bianka NEY, Ágnes RUZSITS, Blanka Csilla TÖRÖK, Erika ZIMÁNYI
Security tasks: Staff members of the Security Department
Technical team: András CZAKÓ, András ELLENBACHER, Zulejka LÁSZLÓ, Rómeó MIKLÓS, Szabolcs MOLNÁR, Sándor NAGYPÁL, Norbert NIEDERKIRCHNER, István PÁZMÁNY, Mihály POZSÁR, Attila SÁNDOR, Zoltán SÜTŐ, Gergő SZILÁGYI, Lajos TOR, Károly UDREA
Friends of the Museum coordination: Krisztina RÉBÉK-SCHAY, Marcell SZTUPKAI

CATALOGUE

Editors: Judit GESKÓ, Anett SOMODI
Associate editor: Dominika SODICS
Copy editors: Noémi BÖRÖCZKI, Steve KANE

Translations: Steve KANE

Editorial coordination: Krisztina SZVOBODA
Reproduction rights: Szilvia CSEH
Catalogue design and pre-press work: Anna FARKAS, anagraphic
Printing: Gyomai Kner Nyomda Zrt., Zoltán CSÖNDES, CEO
Publisher: László BAÁN, General Director
Museum of Fine Arts, Budapest, 2024
ISBN 978-615-6595-48-5

Cover: Pablo Picasso and Jacques Lipchitz in the South of France, ca. 1968
Photo, private collection
Photo © Museum of Fine Arts, Budapest

The editors of the catalogue and the organisers of the exhibition would like to thank to Anne-Sophie KOVÁCS, Rebeka MRÁZIK, Miriam SZŐCS, and Ferenc TÓTH.

Cooperating Partners

Maintainer of the Institution

MINISTRY OF CULTURE
AND INNOVATION